MERRILL Science

AUTHORS

Dr. Jay K. Hackett
University of Northern Colorado

Dr. Richard H. Moyer
University of Michigan-Dearborn

Dr. Donald K. Adams
University of Northern Colorado

Contributing Writer
Ann H. Sankey
Science Specialist
Educational Service District 121
Seattle, Washington

Reading Consultant
Barbara S. Pettegrew, Ph.D.
Director of the Reading/Study Center
Assistant Professor of Education
Otterbein College
Westerville, Ohio

Safety Consultant
Gary E. Downs, Ed.D.
Professor
Iowa State University
Ames, Iowa

Gifted and Mainstreaming Consultants
George Fichter
Educational Consultant
Programs for Gifted
Ohio Department of Education
Worthington, Ohio

Timothy E. Heron, Ph.D.
Professor
Department of Human Services, Education
The Ohio State University
Columbus, Ohio

Primary Levels Consultant
Maureen E. Allen
Science Resource Specialist
Irvine Unified School District
Irvine, California

Content Consultants
Robert T. Brown, M.D.
Associate Professor of Clinical Pediatrics
Director, Section for Adolescent Health
The Ohio State University/Children's Hospital
Columbus, Ohio

Henry D. Drew, Ph.D.
Chemist
U.S. FDA, Division of Drug Analysis
St. Louis, Missouri

Judith L. Doyle, Ph.D.
Physics Teacher
Newark High School
Newark, Ohio

Todd F. Holzman, M.D.
Child Psychiatrist
Harvard Community Health Plan
Wellesley, Massachusetts

Knut J. Norstog, Ph.D.
Research Associate
Fairchild Tropical Garden
Miami, Florida

James B. Phipps, Ph.D.
Professor, Geology/Oceanography
Grays Harbor College
Aberdeen, Washington

R. Robert Robbins, Ph.D.
Associate Professor of Astronomy
Astronomy Department, University of Texas
Austin, Texas

Sidney E. White, Ph.D.
Professor
Department of Geology & Mineralogy
The Ohio State University
Columbus, Ohio

ACKNOWLEDGEMENT

The authors are deeply indebted to the late Robert B. Sund for his inspiration and guidance in the early development of this series.

MERRILL
PUBLISHING COMPANY
A Bell & Howell Information Company
Toronto • London • Sydney

Merrill Science Program Components

Student Editions, K-6
Teacher Editions, K-6
Teacher Resource Books, K-6
    (Reproducible Masters)
Big Books, K-2
SkillBuilders: A Process & Problem Solving
    Skillbook, Student Editions, K-6
SkillBuilders: A Process & Problem Solving
    Skillbook, Teacher Editions, K-6

Poster Packets: Science in Your World, K-6
Color Transparencies, K-6
Activity Materials Kits, K-6
Activity Materials Management System
Awards Stickers
Science Words Software, 1-6
In-service Videotapes
Mr. Wizard Videos, 3-7
Science Fair Package

Dr. Jay K. Hackett is Professor of Earth Science Education at the University of Northern Colorado. He holds a B.S. in General Science, an M.N.S. in Physical Science, and an Ed.D. in Science Education with support in Earth Science. A resource teacher for elementary schools, he conducts numerous workshops and professional seminars. With over 20 years of teaching experience, he has taught and consulted on science programs across all levels and remains active in local, state, and national science professional organizations.

Dr. Richard H. Moyer is Professor of Science Education at the University of Michigan, Dearborn. He holds a B.S. in Chemistry and Physics Education, an M.S. in Curriculum and Instruction, and an Ed.D. in Science Education. With more than 19 years of teaching experience at all levels, he is currently involved in teacher training. He was the recipient of two Distinguished Faculty Awards. He conducts numerous workshops and in-service training programs for science teachers. Dr. Moyer is also the author of Merrill's *General Science* textbook.

Dr. Donald K. Adams is Professor of Education and Director, Education Field Experiences at the University of Northern Colorado. He holds a B.S. in Liberal Arts Social Science, an M.S. in Biological Science, and an Ed.D. in Science Education with support in Earth Science. In over 20 years of teaching, he has been instrumental in implementing personalized science and outdoor education programs and has served as a consultant to teacher preparation and science programs throughout the United States, Australia, and New Zealand.

Reviewers: Teachers and Administrators   Mary Alice Bernreuter, Mae Walters Elementary School, Hialeah, FL; **Virginia Ceruti,** Cleveland Elementary School, Norwood, MA; **Sister Teresa Fitzgerald,** CSJ, Office of Catholic Education, Brooklyn, NY; **JoAnn Hamm,** Danville Board of Education, Danville, KY; **Norma Jones,** Austin Tracy School, Lucas, KY; **Barbara Kmetz,** Trumbull High School, Trumbull, CT; **Corinne Measelle,** Palm Beach County School Board, West Palm Beach, FL; **Waltina Mroczek,** Beachwood Elementary School, Beachwood, OH; **Donald Paul,** Vineland Board of Education, Vineland, NJ; **Peggy Smith,** Special Education Resource Teacher, Fort Worth, TX; **Frank Stone,** Floranada Elementary School, Fort Lauderdale, FL; **Lana Tarlton,** Cook Elementary School, Austin, TX; **John Varine,** Kiski Area School District, Vandergrift, PA; **Dr. Rosa White,** Cutler Ridge Elementary School, Miami, FL

Cover Photo: Tyrannosaurus rex dinosaur by Commercial Image/COSI (Center of Science and Industry, Columbus); Museum of History and Science, Louisville; Science Museums of Charlotte—Discovery Place, Charlotte Museum; and The Science Museums of Connecticut—Maryland Science Center, Museum of Science of Boston
Series Editors: Karen S. Allen, Janet L. Helenthal; **Project Editor:** Shelle R. Thraen; **Editor:** Linda Ashe McLaughlin; **Project Designer:** Joan Shaull; **Series Artist:** Dennis L. Smith; **Project Artist:** Paul Helenthal; **Illustrators:** Kirchoff/Wohlberg, Inc., Jeanine S. Means, Publishers' Graphics, Inc.; **Photo Editor:** Barbara Buchholz; **Series Production Editor:** Joy E. Dickerson; **Project Production Editor:** Annette Hoffman

ISBN 0-675-03512-0

Published by

Merrill Publishing Co.
A Bell & Howell Information Company
Columbus, Ohio 43216

Table of Contents

Chapter 1

Animals Change   2

Chapter 2

Changes on Earth   26

Chapter 5

You Grow and Change 98

Chapter 6

Heat 122

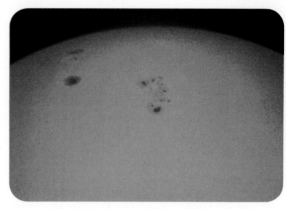

Chapter 7

Changes in the Air 144

Chapter 8

Earth and the Sun 166

Chapter 9

Plants Change   192

Chapter 10

Our Environment Changes   216

Science in Your World

Have you ever held a turtle? What does it eat? Where does it sleep? Using science, you can find out about living things.

Science also can help you learn about change. What did Earth look like many years ago? What do many scientists think happened to the dinosaurs?

Using science, you can solve problems. You can find out how fast the wind is blowing. You can learn how to make your shadow longer.

Think about your world. What questions do you have? Science can help you find the answers.

Chapter 1

Animals Change

All animals are living things. Living things grow and change. What do you know about the way animals grow? How does this animal change?

A Monarch caterpillar

A Monarch butterfly changes as it grows.

Animal Groups

All animals need food, water, and air. There are other ways animals are alike. Some have the same body coverings. Some have the same body parts. Some animals grow and change in the same way.

People who study animals put them in groups. Animals that are most alike are put in the same group. How are these animals alike?

Insects are one animal group. An **insect** has six legs and three main body parts. Many insects have wings.

Insects do not have bones. But, they have a shell. This shell protects the inside parts of their bodies. Have you ever felt the shell of an insect? What did it feel like?

Insects hatch from eggs. Some young insects look like their parents. Other young insects do not look the same as their parents. They change as they grow. These insects go through different stages. Then, they look like their parents.

Look at the changes this insect makes. How many times does it change?

Insects do not need much care. The young protect themselves. They find their own food. Where do insects live?

Activity 1–1

How Do Mealworms Change?

Materials

oatmeal   plastic cup   mealworms
water   hand lens   paper towel
pencil and paper

What to do

1. Put oatmeal in a cup.
2. Put the mealworms on the oatmeal. Cover them with a paper towel.
3. Sprinkle water on the towel every day.
4. Observe for about 3 weeks. Brush away the top layer of oatmeal.
5. Look at the insects with a hand lens.

What did you learn?

1. What happened to the mealworms?
2. How did the body parts change?
3. What other insects change like mealworms?

Fish are a group of animals. Fish live in water. All **fish** have gills. Fish use gills to take in air from water. Why do fish need air?

Most fish have bony skeletons inside their bodies. The skeletons give their bodies shape. Most fish have a wet, scaly skin. They use fins and a tail to move. How do fish use these body parts to move?

Fish lay many eggs. Some of the eggs hatch. The small young fish grow to look like their parents.

Fish Farming

People who catch fish to sell must follow some fishing rules. They must not catch young fish. Young fish need time to grow.

At a fish hatchery, fish eggs are allowed to grow. They grow in large tanks of water. As the fish get bigger, they are taken out of the tanks. The bigger fish are put into oceans or lakes.

A Special Group

Frogs, salamanders, and toads are amphibians. An **amphibian** can live in water and on land. Young amphibians live in water. Their bodies change as they grow. These animals can then live on the land.

Most amphibians have wet, smooth skin. Many live near water. Most have four legs and some also have a tail. They all have bony skeletons.

Amphibians lay many eggs. Only some of the eggs hatch. When the eggs hatch, the young care for themselves. What might happen to the eggs that do not hatch?

These amphibians are frogs. Look
at how frogs grow and change. Young
frogs are called tadpoles. Tadpoles
do not look like their parents. They
hatch from eggs that are laid in water.
Young tadpoles do not have legs.
They use tails to swim. They use gills
to get air from water.

Tadpoles change as they grow. Their tails get shorter. Hind legs start to grow. Then front legs grow. The tadpoles also grow lungs. They slowly change into frogs. The frogs move out of the water. Then they live on land. They use lungs to get air. How do frogs move on land?

Reptiles are another group of animals. Snakes, turtles, lizards, and alligators are reptiles. A **reptile** has dry, scaly skin. It has a bony skeleton that gives its body shape. Most reptiles have four legs and a tail. Which kind of reptile does not have legs? How do you think this kind of reptile moves?

Most reptiles lay eggs. Some reptiles bury their eggs in sand. Some make a nest.

A young reptile grows and changes inside the egg. When a young reptile breaks out of the egg, it looks like its parents. But, it is much smaller. Most young reptiles care for themselves. They protect themselves, too. Think about animals that are reptiles. How does each kind protect itself?

Birds are a group of animals. Every **bird** has feathers and a beak. Most are able to fly. All birds have bony skeletons.

Young birds hatch from eggs. Parent birds lay a few eggs at a time. They keep the eggs warm.

Some birds have their eyes closed when they hatch. Some have no feathers. The feathers grow as the young bird grows. Most parent birds take care of their young. How do you think they do this?

Activity 1–2

How Are Birds Different?

Materials

bird books   pencil and paper
crayons

What to do

1. Look at some books about birds.
2. On your paper, draw a picture of a bird that can be a pet. Color it.
3. Draw a picture of a bird that can swim. Color it.
4. Draw a picture of a bird that lives in the wild. Color it.
5. Write about each bird.

What did you learn?

1. How are your birds alike?
2. How are your birds different?
3. What makes birds different from all other animal groups?

Mammals are a group of animals. A **mammal** has skin that is covered with hair. But, the hair on some mammals is not very thick. All mammals have bony skeletons.

A few mammals live in water. But, most mammals live on land. Some are little, and some are very big. Look at the pictures. These animals are all mammals. What body parts do mammals have?

Most mammals do not lay eggs. Most young mammals grow and change inside their mothers. Then when they are ready, they are born.

Young mammals look like their parents. But, most of them need a lot of care. Parents care for them so they can grow. Young mammals need to be protected. They need to be fed. They feed on milk from their mother. As young mammals grow, they learn to care for themselves.

Activity 1–3

Materials

hand lens
pencil and paper

What to do

1. Take a walk outdoors with your class.
2. Use the hand lens and observe animal tracks.
3. Observe signs that show where animals had something to eat.
4. Observe signs that show where animals live.
5. Write about what you observe.

What did you learn?

1. What animals live near your school?
2. To what groups do these animals belong?
3. How did you find out where animals live?

People and Science

Watch the Birdie!

Have you ever used a camera? When Carol Parker was a child, she got her first camera. She learned to love taking pictures.

Now, Carol is a wildlife photographer. She takes pictures of animals. She must move very quietly so she does not disturb or frighten the animals. What do you think she is taking a picture of now?

Other Changes

Animals change when they grow. They change in other ways, too. Many animals change when the seasons change. When it is hot, some animals need to keep cool. How do some animals keep cool in the summer?

When it is cold, some animals need to keep warm. Some animals store extra fat for winter. This fat keeps their bodies warm. How do birds stay warm in winter? What changes do other animals make for the seasons?

The hair on some animals changes color with the seasons. In winter, this hair turns white like the snow. In summer, this hair is brown. How does this change in color protect some animals?

If animals sense they are in danger, they may change the way they act to protect themselves. Some animals pretend they are not alive. Sometimes this trick fools other animals. How else do they protect themselves?

Chapter 1 Review

Science I Know

- Animals are living things that grow and change.

- We group animals that are most alike.

- Some animal groups are insects, fish, amphibians, reptiles, birds, and mammals.

- Many animals change when the seasons change.

Science Words

Pick the best word for each sentence.

insect fish amphibian reptile bird mammal

1. An animal with six legs is an _____.

2. An _____ lives in water and on land.

3. An animal with feathers is a _____.

4. You are a _____.

5. A turtle is a kind of _____.

6. An animal with fins and gills is a _____.

Questions to Answer

Use the pictures to help answer the questions.

1. How do young animals get food?
2. How does a fish get air in water?
3. How does a frog tadpole grow and change?
4. How do animals use water?
5. How do some mammals change for winter?

Something to Do

Use a 📷. Take pictures of animals that live near you. Study your pictures. Think about where each animal lives. Think about what each animal needs to live. Group the animals in your pictures.

Books to Read

Little Giants by Seymour Simon
Raccoon Baby by Berniece Freschet
The Story of the Dancing Frog by Quentin Blake

Chapter 2

Changes on Earth

Earth has changed. It does not look the same today as it did long ago. How do you think Earth has changed?

Africa today

Dinosaurs lived millions of years ago.

Land and Water

Earth is not the same all over. Land on Earth has different shapes. These land shapes are called **landforms**. Mountains are landforms. Mountains are made of rock.

Some landforms are flat or have small hills. These landforms are called plains. A plain has thick layers of soil.

Another kind of landform is a desert. A desert has very little rain or snow. Many deserts are covered with sand.

Suppose you could visit the landforms in these pictures. What would you see from the top of this mountain? What animals could you see in this desert?

Land covers only some of Earth. Most of Earth is covered by water. A very large body of water is called an ocean. Ocean water is not like water you drink. Ocean water is very salty.

Look at the map of Earth. What parts of the map do you think are water? Does Earth have more ocean water or land?

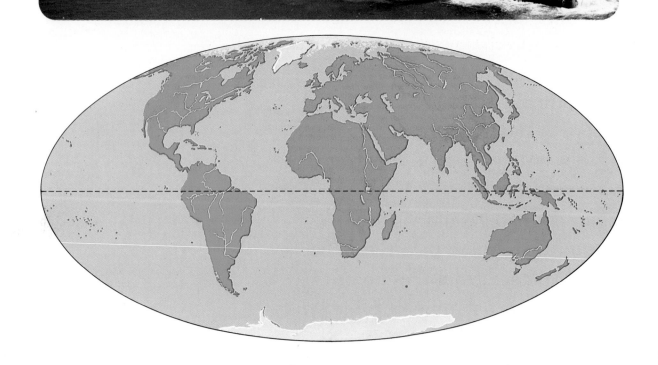

   Some other bodies of water are
lakes and rivers. Most lakes and
rivers are fresh water. Fresh water
does not have much salt. Rain is
fresh water. Fresh water also comes
from snow. Rain and snow run off
mountains and plains. This water
runs into lakes and rivers. Some of
it soaks into the ground. What
bodies of water do you live near?

Earth Changes

Earth is always changing. Wind and water cause changes. Wind picks up soil and sand and moves them to other places. Moving water changes Earth because it carries away rocks and soil.

Glaciers change Earth. A **glacier** is a large body of ice that moves. A glacier moves slowly. It carries away rocks and soil as it moves.

People cause changes on Earth, too. People move rocks and soil to make roads. They cut down trees to make room for buildings. They clear land so they can plant crops.

Sometimes people cause changes they do not want. Large fires may be started when people are careless. What changes are caused by fire?

Some changes on Earth happen very quickly. Some of these changes can be harmful. Earthquakes can happen without warning. Layers of rock slide past one another. This causes parts of Earth to shake. How are earthquakes harmful?

Floods can happen quickly. Floodwaters carry away soil. Where does the floodwater come from? How are floods harmful?

Some changes on Earth happen slowly. Changes in landforms can take a very long time. Some rocks on Earth build up in layers. Soil and mud get pressed together to make rock layers. The rock layers on top press down on other layers below. How many years do you think it took to form these rock layers?

Activity 2–1

How Can You Build a Model of Rock Layers?

Materials

flour   sand   salt   yellow cornmeal
pencil and paper   small scoop
clear plastic cup

What to do

1. Scoop a layer of sand into the bottom of the cup.
2. Next, scoop a layer of salt on top of the sand. Do not mix the layers.
3. Add a layer of cornmeal.
4. Add a layer of flour.

What did you learn?

1. Which layer did you put in the cup first? Which layer did you add last?
2. Pretend you found a bone in the layer of salt. How many layers would be above the bone?
3. Suppose these layers were layers of rock. Which one do you think would be the oldest?

How Old Are These Rocks?

Scientists study layers of rock to try to find their ages. They try to figure out how long it took each rock layer to form. Then, they decide which rock layers are oldest and which are youngest.

Scientists also study prints and animal and plant parts that are buried in rock layers. These help scientists make better guesses at ages of rocks.

Long ago, this dinosaur footprint was buried in the mud. Slowly, the mud was changed to rock. How do you think scientists know that this is a footprint of a dinosaur?

Scientists have found many fossils. A **fossil** is a print or part of plants or animals that lived long ago. Fossils are used to find out about life long ago. Scientists also use fossils to find out about changes on Earth.

Some fossils are prints or parts of animals that lived in oceans. But, scientists have found these kinds of fossils in places where there are no oceans now. What did scientists learn from these fossils?

Fossils also show scientists the kinds of plants that lived long ago. Which one of these fossils was a plant?

Activity 2-2

What Can You Learn from Prints?

A

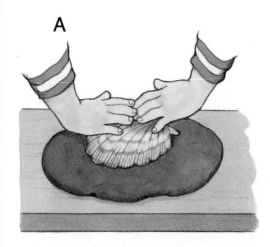

B

Materials

clay	petroleum jelly
hand lens	plaster of paris
shell	pencil and paper
thin cardboard (5 cm by 45 cm)	

What to do

1. Make a ball of clay. Make it flat.
2. Push the shell into the top. See A.
3. Coat the shell and the clay with petroleum jelly.
4. Make a ring with the cardboard strip. Push it into the clay. See B.
5. Pour plaster of paris into the ring. Set it in a safe place to dry.
6. Remove the ring, shell, and clay. Study the print with a hand lens.

What did you learn?

1. How is this print like a real fossil?
2. How is this print different from a real fossil?

Scientists find fossils of dinosaurs. Dinosaurs lived on Earth long ago. Dinosaurs are now extinct. Plants and animals that are **extinct** can no longer be found alive. How do scientists know that dinosaurs are extinct?

Scientists find fossil dinosaur bones. When they put the bones together, they know the size and shape of dinosaurs. How long do you think it takes scientists to put the bones of one dinosaur together?

Scientists have found fossils of dinosaur teeth. The shape and size of the teeth show what dinosaurs ate. Some dinosaurs ate only plants. Their teeth were small and flat. Other dinosaurs ate meat. How do you think their teeth were shaped?

Even fossils of dinosaur eggs have been found. What do you think scientists can find out about dinosaurs from these eggs?

No one knows why dinosaurs became extinct. Scientists know that Earth changed. It may have become very cold. If Earth got colder, what could have happened to plants? Why did dinosaurs need plants?

This sabertooth cat also lived on Earth long ago. Sabertooth cats are now extinct. Some of their fossils are found in tar pits. Sabertooth cats lived after dinosaurs became extinct. The shape of their teeth shows that sabertooth cats ate meat. What animal lives today that looks like sabertooth cats?

Many years later, woolly mammoths lived on Earth. These animals are now extinct, too. Woolly mammoths lived during a time when a large part of Earth was covered with glaciers. Some woolly mammoth fossils have been found frozen in ice. The fossils have large tusks and long hair. What animal do you think looks like woolly mammoths?

The horse is an animal that lived long ago. Horses live on Earth now. But, horses have changed. Scientists have found fossils that show how horses have changed. Some horses that lived long ago were as small as dogs. Horses today are large. Early horses had toes. Horses today have hooves. What did you learn about the way horses have changed?

People and Science

A Dinosaur Builder

Jim Jensen hunts for dinosaur bones. He tries to put them together like pieces of a puzzle. When he cannot find all of the bones for one dinosaur, he makes extra bones out of fiberglass.

Once, Jim found a bone that was 3 meters long. He had to make the rest of the bones. When he fit them altogether, the dinosaur was 30 meters long. The dinosaur was named *Ultrasaurus.*

Chapter 2 Review

- Earth is covered by landforms and water.
- Earth is always changing.
- Some changes on Earth happen quickly. Some changes happen slowly.
- Some plants and animals that lived long ago are extinct.

Science Words

Pick the best word for each sentence.

landforms   glacier   fossil   extinct

1. Scientists learn about life long ago when they find a _____.

2. A plant or animal that can no longer be found alive on Earth is _____.

3. Different shapes of land are called _____.

4. A large body of ice that moves is called a _____.

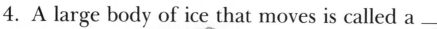

Questions to Answer

Use the picture to help answer the questions.

1. What landforms can you name?
2. How do wind and water change Earth?
3. What changes on Earth happen quickly? Slowly?
4. What are some extinct animals?
5. How do people know about life long ago?

Something to Do

Read about an extinct animal that lived long ago. Make a model of that animal out of clay. Write a story about your extinct animal.

Books to Read

Dinosaurs! A Drawing Book by Michael Emberley
Dinosaurs Are Different by Aliki
Volcanoes by Franklyn M. Branley

Chapter 3

Sound Around Us

Sound is all around us. Some sounds are loud and some are quiet. How do loud sounds make you feel? How do quiet sounds make you feel?

A quiet beach

You hear loud sounds at a circus.

How Is Sound Made?

There are many ways to make sound. One way is by using your voice to talk. What other sounds can you make with your voice?

Sounds are also made in other ways. The wind makes sound. Cars and machines make sounds, too. What sounds do animals make? What are your favorite sounds?

The people in the picture are making sounds. They are using instruments to make music. Each instrument makes a different sound. What sound do you think each instrument makes?

Objects must move back and forth quickly to make sound. We say objects **vibrate** when they move back and forth. They may vibrate so quickly, you cannot see them move.

People can make objects vibrate. Each picture shows something that is making sound. Tell about the pictures. What vibrates to make each sound?

Activity 3–1

How Can You Observe Something Vibrate?

Materials

shoe box   pencil and paper
scissors
3 rubber bands (different sizes)

What to do

1. Carefully cut 3 small slits on each end of the shoe box.
2. Stretch each rubber band around the box.
3. Tuck each rubber band into the slits you made.
4. Pluck the rubber bands.
5. Draw a picture of what you observe.

What did you learn?

1. What happened when you plucked on the rubber bands?
2. What kinds of sounds do different rubber bands make?
3. What are some instruments that use strings to make sounds?

Sounds Move

Sounds move. Most of the sounds you hear move through air. The sound of a bell moves through air. When someone rings a bell, the bell vibrates. The air around the bell vibrates, too.

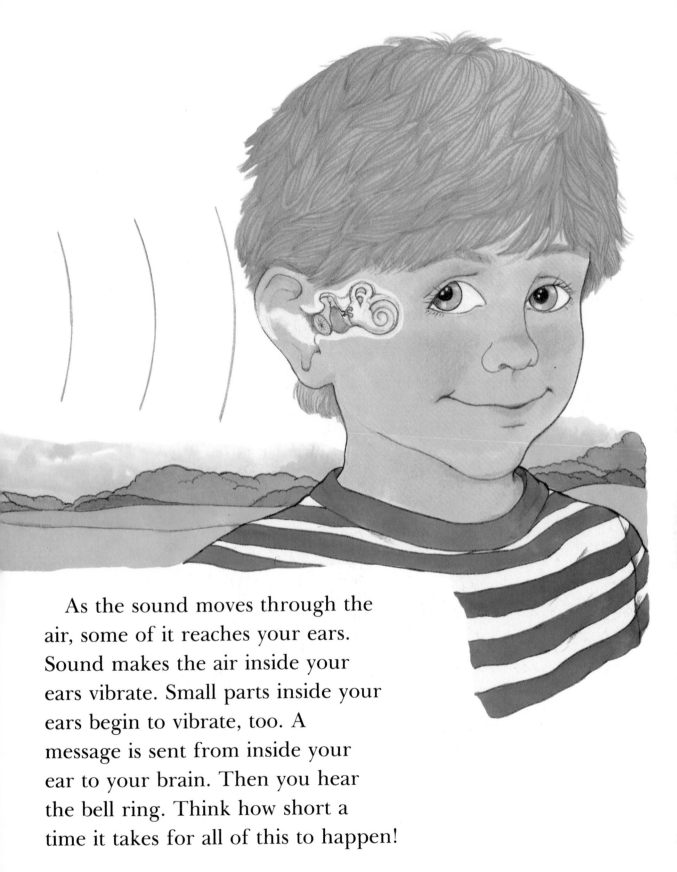

As the sound moves through the air, some of it reaches your ears. Sound makes the air inside your ears vibrate. Small parts inside your ears begin to vibrate, too. A message is sent from inside your ear to your brain. Then you hear the bell ring. Think how short a time it takes for all of this to happen!

You know sounds can move through air. Air is a gas. Sounds can move through solids, too. The children in the picture can talk to each other using a string telephone. What solid does the sound move through on their telephone?

Sounds can also move through water. Water is a liquid. Sounds move through solids, liquids, and gases.

Activity 3-2

How Does a String Telephone Work?

Materials

foam cups
tape
string (3 meters)
pencil and paper

What to do

1. Use your pencil. Make a small hole in the bottom of each cup.
2. Put the ends of the string through the holes.
3. Tape the string to the inside bottom of each cup.
4. Give one cup to a friend. Move apart until the string is tight. Do not touch the string.
5. Listen to your friend talk into the cup.

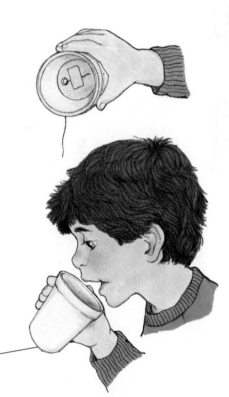

What did you learn?

1. What did you hear in your cup?
2. Through what did the sounds move?
3. What happens to the sound if you touch the string?

59

Sounds Are Different

Many different sounds are made each day. These sounds are all around us.

Some sounds are loud. Fire trucks make loud sounds. Their sirens wail as they race to fires. Loud sounds are easy to hear.

Some sounds are soft. When you walk on tiptoe, you make soft sounds. If you write on paper, your pencil makes soft sounds. You must listen carefully to hear soft sounds. What other soft sounds can you make?

Activity 3-3

Materials

empty soft drink bottles
wooden spoon
water
pencil and paper

What to do

1. Put a different amount of water in each bottle.
2. Carefully tap each bottle with the spoon. Observe what you hear.
3. Put the bottles in order from the lowest to the highest sound.
4. See if you can play a song on your bottles.

What did you learn?

1. Which bottle had the highest sound?
2. Which bottle had the lowest sound?
3. How can you change the sound each bottle makes? Try it.

Look at the bells. The biggest bell makes the lowest sound. The smallest bell makes the highest sound. Sounds can be high or low. The highness or lowness of a sound is called **pitch.** Objects that vibrate very quickly make sounds with a high pitch. Objects that do not vibrate as quickly make sounds with a lower pitch.

People can make high or low
pitched sounds with their voices.
How does the pitch of your voice
change when you sing?

This boy is making sounds with
the glasses of water. The glass with
the most water has the lowest pitch.
Which glass has the highest pitch?

People and Science

Singing Can Be Work

Plácido Domingo is an opera singer. An opera is a play where the characters sing all of the parts. Plácido and other opera singers spend much time practicing for each opera.

Opera singers must protect their voices. They must avoid catching cold. On a day when Plácido has to perform in an opera, he rests his voice. He does not talk until his performance.

Some sounds are pleasant. People like to hear pleasant sounds.

There are other sounds people may not like to hear. Look at the girl. Why is she holding her hands over her ears?

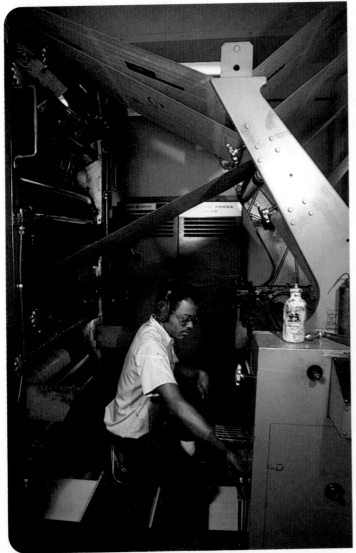

CAUTION

HEARING PROTECTION REQUIRED HERE

Most people do not like to hear loud sounds. Loud sounds can be harmful. Sounds that are too loud can hurt parts of our ears.

The men in the pictures work near very loud sounds. What do they wear over their ears? How does the sign warn people?

Sound that is not pleasant to hear is called **noise.** Where is it noisy in your school? How does the noise make you feel? Maybe you can help stop some noise. You can talk quietly. You can walk quietly in the hall. How can you get other people to help stop noise?

Listening for Loons

Have you ever heard a bird laugh? Loons are birds that sound like they are laughing. Some loons also yodel. Each yodel is different from any other yodel.

Scientists make recordings of loon yodels and other loon calls. They want to find out if loons return to the same lakes and ponds each year. How do you think the recordings will help them?

Many sounds are useful to people. Talking is a useful sound. We can tell other people what we are thinking by talking.

Some useful sounds warn people of danger. Warning sounds can be loud. Pretend you are walking down the street. What sounds could warn you of danger?

Many machines make useful sounds. Telephones and radios make useful sounds. The pictures show objects that make sounds. Tell how the sounds are useful to you. What other sounds do you use?

Chapter 3 Review

- There are many different ways to make sound.
- Sounds are made when objects vibrate.
- Sounds move through solids, liquids, and gases.
- Sounds that are too loud can be harmful.
- Sounds can be useful.

Science Words

Pick the best word for each sentence.

vibrate   pitch   noise

1. The highness or lowness of sound is called _____.

2. When objects move back and forth quickly, they _____.

3. Sound that is not pleasant to hear is _____.

Use the picture to help answer the questions.

1. What objects are making sounds?

2. What vibrates when objects make sounds?

3. Which sounds are soft? Which sounds are loud?

4. Which sounds are high? Which sounds are low?

5. Through what does each sound move?

6. How are the sounds useful?

Something to Do

Have someone help you record different sounds. Play the tape for a friend. Let your friend guess what makes each sound.

Books to Read

All about Sound by David C. Knight
Mystery on the Docks by Thacher Hurd
What's That Noise? by Michele Lemieux

Chapter 4

You Can Measure

People need to measure. They need to measure to find out about our world. They use different instruments to measure. What do you think scientists find out when they measure?

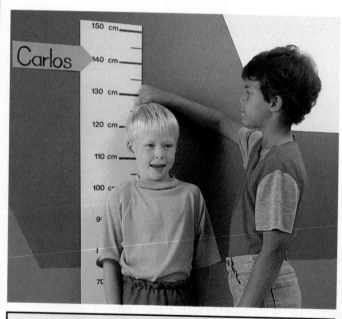

Measuring how tall

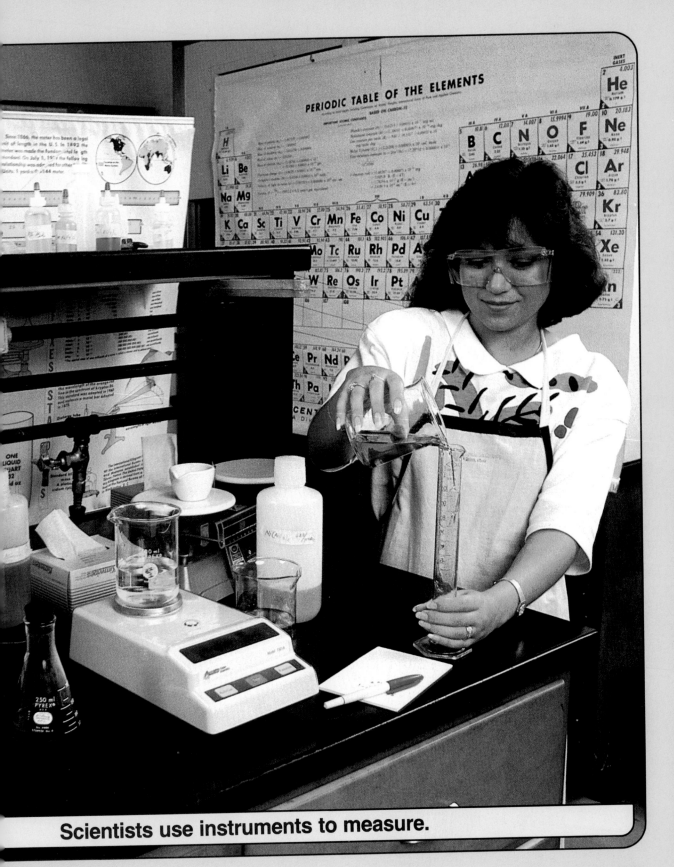

Scientists use instruments to measure.

Learning to Measure

Scientists often measure to find out the sizes of objects. Sometimes they need to know how long or how heavy objects are. They need to know how much some objects hold.

Scientists observe and measure to find out how objects are alike or different. They record what they measure. Then they tell about what they discover.

You can learn to measure. You can learn to record what you measure. You can share what you discover.

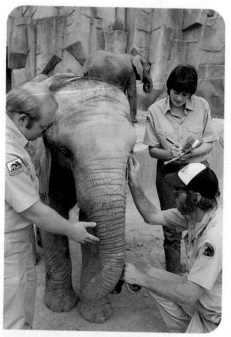

People measure by using units. A unit means one. When people measure, they count units. Any object can be a unit.

Long ago, people used their hands as units of measure. Some people still use hands to measure how tall horses are. Try to measure your desk with your hands. How many hands high is your desk?

You can also use paper clips as units of measure. Choose a book to measure. Place paper clips end to end along one side of your book. Then count the paper clips. How many paper clips long is your book?

Count the paper clips in these chains. Which chain has the most units? Which chain is the longest?

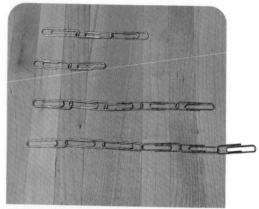

Activity 4–1

How Can You Measure?

Materials

paper clip chain   5 straw parts
pencil and paper

What to do

1. Place the straws in order from shortest to longest.
2. Measure the shortest straw with the paper clip chain. Record how many paper clips long it is.
3. Guess how many paper clips long the other straws are. Record your guesses.
4. Measure each of the other straws. Record how many paper clips long each straw is.

What did you learn?

1. How many times did you guess right?
2. How did you know what number to guess?
3. What unit did you use to measure the straws?

What happens if people do not use the same size unit to measure objects? Think about this. Suppose two different people measure the same object with their hands. One person might have small hands and say that the object is seven hands long. The other person might have bigger hands and say that the object is five hands long. Who would be right? Why?

People need to use the same size unit to measure objects. They need to agree on what unit to use. There are many units of measure that people have agreed to use.

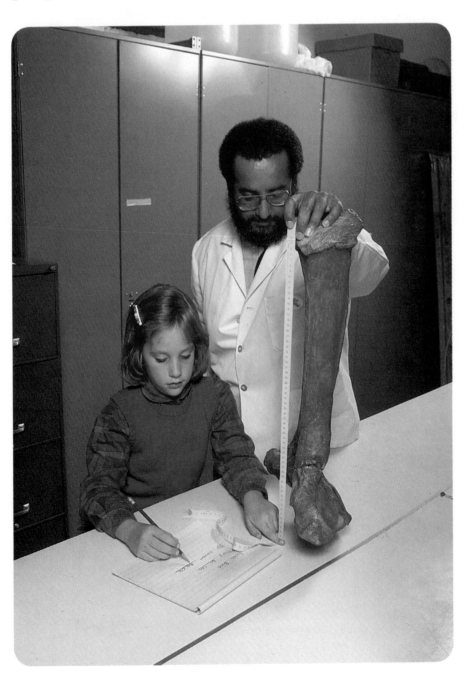

How Long?

One unit that is used all over the world is the centimeter. The **centimeter** is used to measure how long or how wide something is. One centimeter is about the size of one raisin. One centimeter is this long 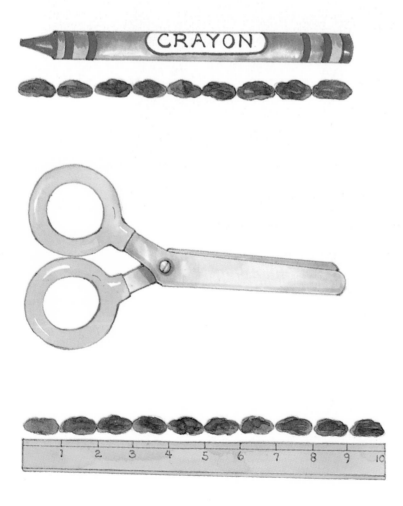 How many centimeters long is each object below?

Activity 4-2

How Can You Measure with Centimeters?

Materials

box of small objects to measure
centimeter ruler   pencil and paper

What to do

1. Choose one object from the box. Place it on your paper.
2. Write the name of the object on your paper.
3. Hold the object. Make a pencil mark on the paper at each end of the object.
4. Use your ruler to measure how many centimeters there are between the marks. Record the number next to the name of the object.
5. Measure the other objects. Record your measurements.

What did you learn?

1. Which object is the longest?
2. Which object is the shortest?

Suppose you want to measure something big. If you use centimeter units, you might find big objects hard to measure. Try it and see. How could using a larger unit be helpful?

A **meter** is a larger unit of measure than a centimeter. It is also used to measure how long or how wide something is. A meter stick is one meter long. There are 100 centimeters in one meter. What can you measure with a meter stick?

Science and Technology

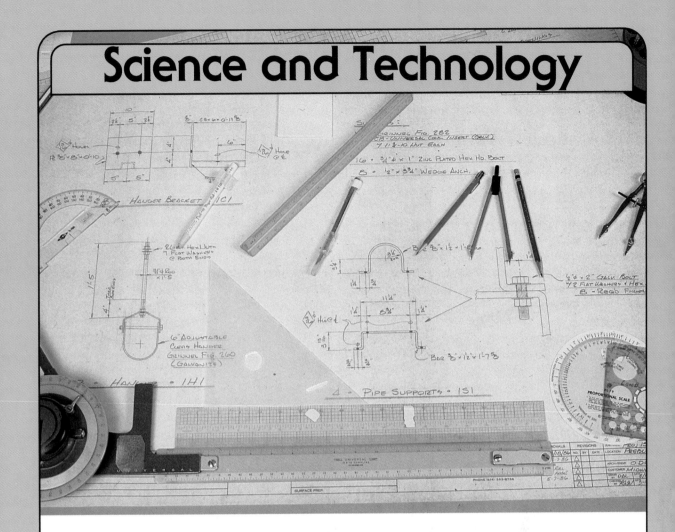

A Measuring Plan

Have you ever seen a blueprint? It is a drawing of a plan to build something. Blueprints for a house show workers how to put each part of that house together.

Each measurement on a blueprint must be exactly right. Workers follow a blueprint to measure and cut parts. What would happen if a measurement was wrong?

How Much?

Which glass can hold the most milk? Which basket can hold the most apples? **Volume** is a measure of how much an object holds. Each glass has a small volume. Each basket has a larger volume.

Look at these containers. Which one could hold the most? Point to them in order from the one with the smallest volume to the largest. See if someone in your class can name a container that has great volume!

Activity 4-3

How Can You Measure Volume?

Materials

small paper cup   dry cereal
pencil and paper   pan
plastic bowl

What to do

1. Use the paper cup as a measuring unit. Fill the cup with cereal.
2. Pour the cereal into the pan. Guess how many more units it will take to fill the pan. Write your guess.
3. Use the cup to fill the pan. Write the number of units.
4. Guess how many cup units will fill the bowl. Write your guess.
5. Use the cup to fill the bowl. Write the number.

What did you learn?

1. How many units did the pan hold?
2. How many units did the bowl hold?
3. Which has the larger volume?

We need units to measure volume, too. A **liter** is a unit that is used to measure volume. A liter is used to find out how much something can hold.

Look at these pictures. The bottle holds about one liter of orange juice. The carton holds about two liters of milk. How can you find out how many liters a pail holds?

People and Science

The Right Measure

Lee Chang is a pharmacist. He prepares the medicines that doctors tell us we need. Lee measures each drug carefully. Then he writes the directions that tell customers how to take each medicine. Lee explains the directions to each customer. He knows that people must take the right amount of medicine for it to make them well.

Sometimes we need to know how heavy something is. **Weight** is a measure of how heavy an object is. How can you measure weight?

A **scale** is an instrument used to measure weight. There are many kinds of scales. What kind of scale can you use to measure your weight? What other kinds of scales have you seen?

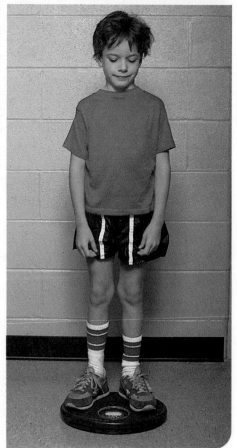

Activity 4–4

How Do You Use a Scale?

Materials

chalk   mesh bag   2 small apples
thick rubber band   10 bags of beans

What to do

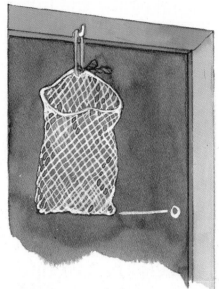

1. Your teacher will hang a rubber band from the top of the chalkboard. Tie the mesh bag to the rubber band.
2. Mark a zero on the chalkboard where the mesh bag ends. Add a bag of beans to the mesh bag. Write number one where the mesh bag ends.
3. Add the other bags of beans one at a time. Number where the mesh bag ends each time. Take out the beans.
4. Put an apple in the mesh bag. Mark where the mesh bag ends.
5. Add the other apple. Mark where the mesh bag ends.

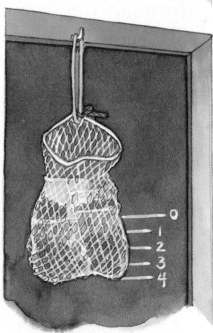

What did you learn?

1. How many bean bag units did the apples weigh?
2. What unit did you use to measure weight?

Measuring Time

You can measure time in large and small units. Time is how long it takes for something to happen. A year is a large unit of time. The time from your last birthday to your next birthday is one year. Tell what the name of this year is. In what year were you born?

A day is a smaller unit of time. There are 365 days in one year. A day has 24 hours. An hour is a smaller unit of time than a day. If you are in school for six hours, how many hours are you away from school each day?

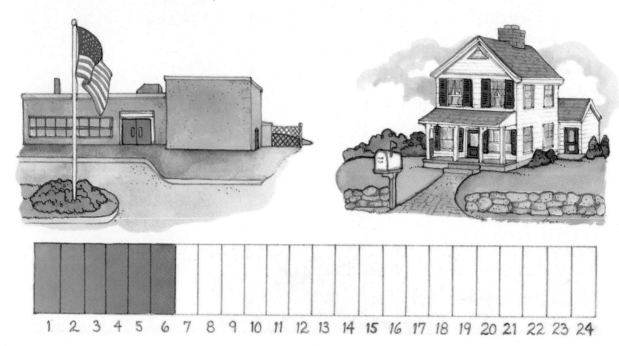

Each hour is made up of smaller units of time called minutes. There are 60 minutes in one hour. A minute is a short unit of time. What can you do in one minute? Can you stand on one foot for a minute? Try it and see.

There are units of time smaller than a minute. One of these units is called a second. There are 60 seconds in one minute. If you count to three quickly, you will use about one second of time. What could you measure in seconds?

Activity 4–5

How Much Time to Change?

Materials

seltzer tablet   banana   ice cube
2 plastic plates   classroom clock
1 jar with water   pencil and paper

What to do

1. Observe your teacher putting the tablet in the jar of water.
2. Measure the time it takes for the tablet to dissolve. Record the time. Record the changes you observe.
3. Put the ice cube on a plate. Check every 15 minutes. Observe how long it takes for the ice to melt. Record the time. Record the changes.
4. Place the banana on the other plate. Observe the banana for 5 days.
5. Record the changes you observe.

What did you learn?

1. How long did it take for each change to happen?
2. What units of time did you use?
3. What other changes can you measure with time?

Chapter 4 Review

Science I Know

- People measure to find out how objects are alike or different.
- We can measure how long objects are.
- We can measure volume or weight.
- Time is a measure of how long it takes for something to happen.

Science Words

Pick the best word for each sentence.

centimeter   meter   volume   liter   weight   scale

1. A measure of how much something holds is called _____.

2. A unit smaller than the meter is a _____.

3. A unit used to measure volume is the _____.

4. We measure how heavy an object is with a _____.

5. A larger unit than the centimeter is the _____.

6. A scale measures _____.

Questions to Answer

Use the pictures to help answer the questions.

1. Why do people use the same units to measure?

2. What can you use to measure how long?

3. Why do you measure volume?

4. What instrument measures weight?

5. What units can you use to measure time?

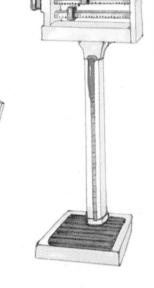

Something to Do

Find out how things are measured in your home. What needs to be measured? What measuring instruments are used? What units are used? Make a list.

Books to Read

Measuring by R. L. Allington and Kathleen Krull
Spaces, Shapes, and Sizes by Jane Jonas Srivastava
Time and Clocks by Herta S. Breiter

Chapter 5

You Grow and Change

All living things grow. They change as they grow. You are living. How are you like other living things?

Learning to play catch

Everybody changes as they grow.

Growing and Changing

How did you look when you were a baby? How do you look now? People change in many ways as they grow.

When you were a baby, you were very small. Your bones and muscles were very small. Other parts of your body were small, too.

As a baby, you could not walk or talk. You needed help to eat. But, you began to change and grow quickly. You learned to move in different ways. You learned to do many things.

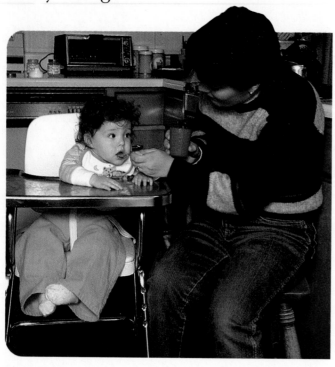

You are growing and changing. Your muscles get stronger. Your bones grow longer. Even your brain changes as you grow. You learn more new things. How can you tell when you have grown?

As you grow older, you will not change and grow as quickly. Your body will keep changing. But, most changes will happen more slowly. What changes do you think will happen slowly?

Activity 5–1

How Have You Grown?

Materials

growth chart   baby records
graph paper   pencil and paper
red and blue crayons

What to do

1. Find out how tall you were as a baby.
2. Have your teacher tell you how many centimeters this is. Color that many boxes on your paper in red.
3. Find out how tall you are now.
4. Color that many boxes on your paper in blue.
5. Count how many more blue boxes there are than red.

What did you learn?

1. How many centimeters have you grown since you were a baby?
2. Who has grown the most in your class?
3. How tall do you think you will be?

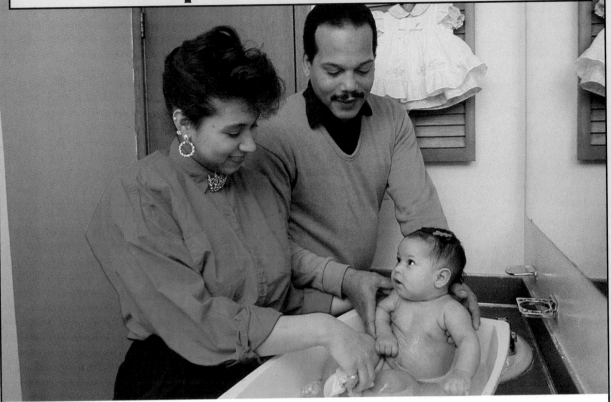

A Job Full of Love

Parents watch children carefully as they grow and change. As babies learn to sit up, crawl, and walk, parents look for special changes. If a baby does not crawl by a certain age, parents may call a doctor.

Think of how much your parents do for you. They want to make sure you grow up strong and healthy. How long do you think this job of your parents will last?

Growing Teeth

Your teeth grow and change. Most people grow two different sets of teeth. The first set of teeth is called **baby teeth.** Baby teeth begin to grow when you are about six months old. Ten baby teeth grow in the top part of your mouth. How many do you think grow in the bottom part? What do babies learn as their teeth grow?

Baby teeth are small and hard.
You start to lose these teeth when
you are about six years old. A second
set of teeth called **permanent teeth**
grows in their place.

Permanent teeth are different
from baby teeth. It takes a few
years for all of them to grow in.
They are bigger and harder.
Permanent teeth will need to last
the rest of your life. You will grow
16 permanent teeth in the top part
of your mouth. How many do you
think grow in the bottom part?

Growing and Learning

People learn as they grow and change. People learn skills. A **skill** is learning how to do something well. Learning to read and write are skills. What other skills do people learn? What skills do you want to learn as you grow up?

There are many things to learn. You can choose what to learn. You can learn to make music. You can be an artist. You can try many different sports.

At first it is hard to learn a new skill. You have to learn new ways to move your body. You must practice and practice. Then, one day you know how to do that skill well. Learning to do something well can make you feel good about yourself.

Activity 5–2

How Can You Learn Something New?

Materials

library books or resource person
objects needed for skill
pencil and paper

What to do

1. Choose a new skill to learn.
2. Gather all of the objects you will need to learn the skill you choose.
3. Follow directions from a book or have someone teach you the skill.
4. Plan how long you will practice this new skill each day.
5. Practice the skill for one week.

What did you learn?

1. What new skill did you learn to do?
2. How much more practice do you think you need?
3. What other new skill would you like to learn?

You may learn to do something because your family likes to do it. If your family likes to go camping, you may learn how to camp. You may learn to like a special kind of music because your family likes it.

Sometimes what people learn depends on where they live. People who live near mountains may learn to ski. People who live near water may learn to swim. What have you learned because of where you live?

Learning to do something can make you feel special. But, you are special because there is no one else just like you. You may look like someone in your family. You may have the same color eyes as your mother. You may have the same kind of nose as your father. But, no two people are alike in every way. Even twins are different.

   Look around your classroom.
How are the people in your class
alike? How are they different?

   People can be different in many
ways. Their hair can be a different
color. They may be different sizes.
Everyone has different fingerprints.

   There is a part of you that is
different from everyone else. That
is what makes you special! What is
special about you?

Growing Up Healthy

Growing and changing bodies need energy. **Energy** makes you able to work and play. You need energy to read. You need energy to run.

Your body needs energy to build strong bones and muscles. Food gives you energy to grow. Healthful food builds a strong, healthy body. What kinds of food are healthful?

Your body needs fruits and vegetables every day. Your body needs milk or cheese, meat, and grains. What foods are made from grains?

Breakfast is an important time to eat. A good breakfast gives you energy to learn and to play. What did you have for breakfast today?

Your body needs exercise to be healthy. **Exercise** keeps muscles strong. Your body grows better when you exercise. What can you do to exercise?

Your body needs rest to stay healthy. When you rest, your muscles relax. Other parts of your body slow down. Your whole body has time to build up energy for another day. How many hours do you rest each day?

Keeping your body clean will help it stay healthy. Hot, soapy water kills germs that can make you sick. [1]What do you do each day to keep yourself clean?

Your teeth need to stay clean, too. Brush your teeth so that germs cannot hurt your teeth. How can brushing your teeth keep your body healthy?

Growing Up Safely

To stay healthy, you must stay safe. To be safe, you must think about what you are planning to do before you do it. You must learn to be careful.

You can learn to play safely. On the playground, you can learn to climb safely. You can learn safe ways to use the swings.

At home, you can find safe ways to play. Would it be safe to play with sharp objects? What ways can you think of to play safely?

You need to think about being safe at other times. Playing with matches is not safe. Playing near a hot stove is not safe. You even need to be careful when you use electricity. What could happen if you are not careful?

You need to be careful using medicine. Your doctor knows when you need medicine. Your parents know too. Do not take any medicine unless a parent or doctor gives it to you. Why do you need to be careful with medicine?

There are other times to think of safety. When you ride a bike, you need to practice safe bicycle rules. What are some safety rules for riding a bicycle?

There are safety rules to obey when you cross a street. Remember to look both ways before you cross. Remember to walk in the crosswalk.

You must even be safe when you ride in a car. You must wear a seat belt. Seat belts can keep you safe if an accident happens. Remember to wear one when you ride in a car.

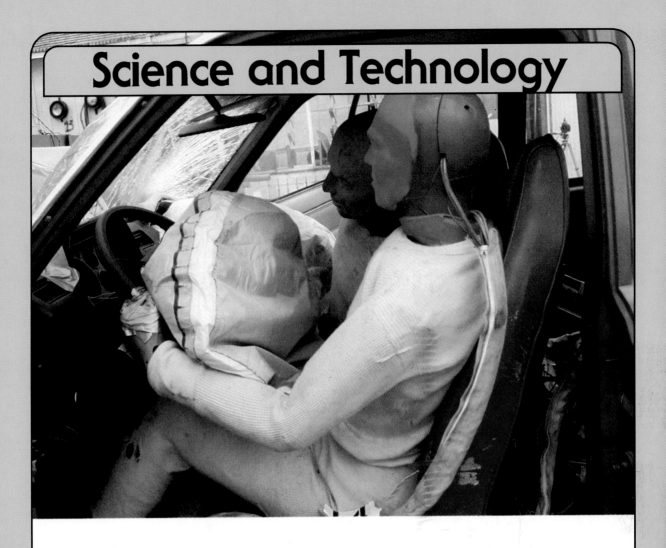

Crash Protection

Scientists test cars to find ways to keep people safer. They use life-size dummies and crash the cars. Scientists study the safety equipment to see if the dummies are protected.

Many tests were done with dummies wearing seat belts. Other tests were done with dummies not wearing seat belts. The tests proved that seat belts keep people safer in cars.

Chapter 5 Review

Science I Know

- People change as they grow.
- As you grow, you learn new skills.
- You are like your parents and you are different from them.
- You can grow up in healthy ways.

Science Words

Pick the best word for each sentence.

baby teeth   permanent teeth   skill   energy   exercise

1. You must practice to learn a new _____.
2. Healthful food gives you _____ to grow.
3. Your first set of teeth is _____.
4. You need _____ to grow and change in a healthy way.
5. The second set of teeth is _____.

Questions to Answer

Use the picture to help answer the questions.

1. How do you change as you grow?
2. When are you too old to learn a new skill?
3. How are people alike?
4. How are people different?
5. How can people stay healthy?

Something to Do

Make people puppets from paper bags. Some puppets could be babies, and some could be older. Write a play for your puppets.

Books to Read

Grandpa and Bo by Kevin Henkes
Helping Out by George Ancona
Someone Special Just Like You by Tricia Brown

Chapter 6

Heat

Heat is all around you. You can feel heat. How does heat make you feel when you are warm? How does heat make you feel when you are cold?

Cooling off

People keep warm on winter evenings with cozy fires.

Heat Moves

Heat causes objects to feel warm. Try rubbing your hands together. Feel the heat. The faster you rub, the more heat you feel. What happens to the heat when you move your hands apart?

The heat from your hands moves. It moves to cooler parts of your hands. It also moves into the air. Heat always moves from warmer objects to cooler ones. We cannot see heat move, but we can feel it.

Activity 6–1

How Does Heat Move?

Materials

bowl of warm water
bowl of ice water
bowl of water at room temperature
pencil and paper

What to do

1. Put your left hand into the bowl of warm water.
2. At the same time, put your right hand into the ice water.
3. Move both hands into the bowl of water that is at room temperature.

What did you learn?

1. How did your left hand feel after you moved it?
2. How did your right hand feel after you moved it?
3. How did the heat move in each of your hands?

Pretend you are standing near a cozy fire on a cold day. Heat from the fire would move and warm the air around it. The warm air would then make you feel warm. When heat moves, it can make people and objects warmer.

Science and Technology

Energy from the Sun

When we use the sun to heat something for us, we are using solar energy. Scientists have learned how to use solar energy to heat buildings.

In a solar collector panel, a liquid such as water is moved through pipes. Heat from the sun warms the water in these pipes. The warm water is pumped to other parts of the building. It can be used for washing or heating.

Heat Causes Change

Heat can change objects in different ways. Some objects may change with a little heat. Other objects may not change until they get very hot. How have you observed changes caused by heat?

When some objects get warmer, they melt. Think about butter. Butter melts when it gets warm. Butter changes when it melts. How do crayons change if they get too warm? Why does ice cream melt?

Some objects seem to disappear when heat is added. Have you ever wondered what happens to the water in puddles? The water seems to disappear. Heat changes the water. The water goes into the air. What happens when someone boils water? What do you observe about the boiling water?

Most objects get bigger when heat is added. Even air takes up more space when it gets warmer. When the air inside a balloon gets warmer, the air takes up more space. The balloon gets bigger. How does heat change the air inside the balloon? How does this air change the balloon?

Activity 6-2

How Can Heat Cause Change?

Materials

empty soft drink bottle
balloon

What to do

1. Fit the balloon onto the neck of the bottle.
2. Put the bottle with the balloon in a sunny spot on the windowsill.
3. Observe what happens.
4. Move the bottle to a cooler spot away from heat.
5. Observe what happens.

What did you learn?

1. How did the balloon change?
2. What caused the changes?
3. Tell about other ways heat can cause changes.

Heat from the Sun

Most of the heat on Earth comes from the sun. Heat from the sun is very important. The heat from the sun warms Earth. Without the sun, Earth would freeze. Living things would die.

All living things need heat. Heat from the sun helps keep animals warm. Some animals need to stay warmer than others. Some animals live where it is warm all year long. Other animals move to warm places when the weather turns cold.

Plants need heat from the sun.
Heat from the sun warms the soil
and the air. This helps plants grow.
Some plants grow only where it is
warm all year long. Which plants
do you think grow only in
warmer places? Which plants grow
where it is cold?

Making and Using Heat

Heat is made when an object burns. An object that is burned to make heat is called a **fuel**. People use different fuels to make heat. Natural gas and oil are fuels. They are burned to heat many homes and buildings. Some buildings are heated by burning coal. Coal is a fuel, too.

Coal, oil, and natural gas can be used to make electricity. Electricity can then be used to make heat. Some homes are heated with electricity. How is your home heated?

Electricity is used to make heat for other objects in your home. How do we use heat in the objects in the pictures? What other objects use electricity to make heat?

People use heat in other ways. Heat is used to cook food. Most stoves and ovens make heat from electricity or natural gas. What other ways can food be cooked?

Have you ever taken a bath in cold water? How did it feel? Many homes have water that is heated. The water is heated by natural gas or electricity. It is stored in hot water tanks. Then people use the hot water as they need it.

People and Science

Special Delivery

John Murphy works for an oil company. John delivers oil to heat homes and other buildings. He pumps the oil from his truck to basement storage tanks. Then the oil is burned to heat water or air to warm buildings.

John also cleans and repairs oil burners so they work better. Oil burners that work better may use less oil. This helps people save oil and money!

Temperature

Temperature is a measure of how warm something is. An object that is warm has a high temperature. An object that is cold has a low temperature. Does a snowflake have a high or a low temperature?

Temperatures can change. If an object gets hotter, its temperature gets higher. If an object gets colder, its temperature gets lower. How could you measure the temperature of an object?

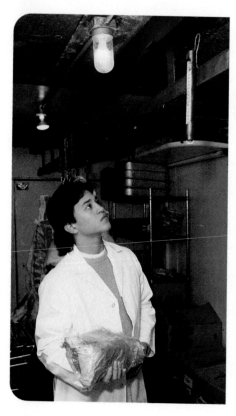

People use a thermometer to measure the temperature of an object. A **thermometer** measures how cold or hot an object is. There are different kinds of thermometers.

One kind is a glass tube. A liquid is in the tube. Heat causes the liquid in the tube to change. The liquid takes up more space when it gets warmer. The liquid takes up less space when it gets cooler.

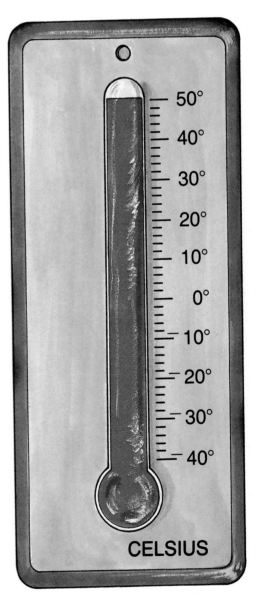

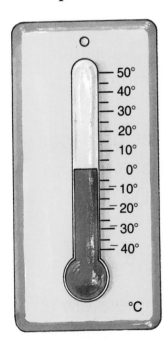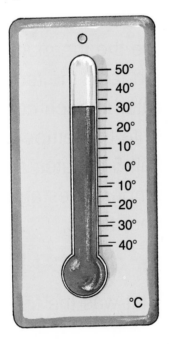

People read thermometers by counting units. A unit on a thermometer is called a **degree**. How many degrees do you read on these thermometers?

Activity 6–3

What Is the Temperature?

Materials

thermometer   ice cubes   water
2 clear cups   clock
pencil and paper

What to do

1. Fill 1 cup with water and ice cubes.
2. Fill the other cup with warm water.
3. Use the thermometer. Measure and read the temperature of the water in each cup.
4. Write the temperatures on paper.
5. Wait 5 minutes and take the temperatures again. Do this 2 more times.

What did you learn?

1. What was the first temperature of the warm water? The ice water?
2. What happened to the temperature of the ice water? The warm water?
3. How did heat move in the ice water? The warm water?

People measure temperatures. They use different kinds of thermometers for different objects. Which thermometer measures body temperature? Which one measures the temperature of the air outside? Why might people record temperatures?

Chapter 6 Review

════════════Science I Know════════════

- Heat always moves from warmer places or objects to cooler ones.

- Heat causes objects to change.

- The sun is the most important way we get heat.

════════════Science Words════════════

Pick the best word for each sentence.

heat   fuel   temperature   thermometer   degree

1. How hot or cold an object is can be measured with a _____.

2. A _____ is burned to make heat.

3. Objects feel warm because of _____.

4. A unit on a thermometer is a _____.

5. We call a measure of how warm something is its _____.

Questions to Answer

Use the picture to help answer the questions.

1. Where does heat come from?
2. How does heat change objects?
3. How do living things use heat?
4. Why do people measure heat?

Something to Do

Try this recipe. You must have an older person help you.

Baked Apples	
4 Apples	4 Tablespoons butter
$\frac{1}{4}$ cup brown sugar	$\frac{3}{4}$ cup hot water

Remove apple cores without cutting all the way through the bottom. Fill each apple with brown sugar. Top with butter. Pour hot water into a pan. Place apples, upright, in pan. Cover. Bake at 375° for 45 minutes.

Books to Read

Fire by John Satchwell
Heat by Laurence Santrey
Hot and Cold by Neil Ardley

Chapter 7

Changes in the Air

Air is all around us. Sometimes you can feel air and hear it move. When can you feel air? When can you hear it move?

Windy weather

Moving air keeps kites flying high.

Air and Weather

Air is a layer of gases around Earth. It covers Earth like a thick blanket. Air reaches from the ground to high above Earth. There is even air in soil and water.

146

Air outside is always changing. It can be warm or cold. It may feel dry or wet. Air may move slowly or very fast. Sometimes it may seem like it is not moving at all.

Changes in the air can happen slowly or quickly. What changes have you observed in the air today? What changes have you observed in the air this week?

147

Changes in the air cause weather. **Weather** is what is happening in the air outdoors. Weather is always changing because air is always changing.

People observe weather. People learn how to tell what kind of weather to expect when some changes happen. What do you think the weather will be tomorrow? How can you find out what to expect?

People and Science

Flying with the Wind

Louis Scott is a pilot. Changes in the air are important to Louis. He has to keep track of storms so he can avoid them when he is flying.

Louis uses the instruments on the flight panel of his plane to help him plan his flights. He can tell how long a flight will take by knowing wind speed and direction. Louis never misses a weather report when he is getting ready to fly.

Wind and Weather

In which picture is the air moving? How can you tell? Moving air is called **wind**. The wind pushes on things and makes some of them move. You can feel wind push against you. Sometimes, you can see papers and leaves move when the wind blows. Then you can tell which way the wind is blowing.

Wind comes from different directions. Wind coming from the east is called an east wind. Wind coming from the south is called a south wind. What is a wind from the west called?

A **wind vane** shows wind direction. It points to the direction from which the wind is coming. Look at the wind vane in the picture. From which direction is the wind blowing?

Activity 7–1

How Can You Make a Wind Vane?

Materials

straw   2 cutouts   pencil and paper
tape   straight pin   pencil with eraser

What to do

1. Tape a cutout to one end of the straw.
2. Tape the other cutout to the other end of the straw.
3. Carefully push a pin through the middle of the straw.
4. Carefully push the pin into the eraser of the pencil.
5. Hold your wind vane outdoors in the wind. Observe which way the wind vane points.

What did you learn?

1. Which way did your wind vane point?
2. From which way was the wind blowing?
3. How fast was the wind blowing?

Wind Chart	
Name	**What You Observe**
Light Winds	Wind vane points the way from which the wind is blowing. Leaves and twigs move. Kites fly. Umbrellas are hard to hold.
Strong Winds	It is hard to walk. Twigs break off trees. Things blow off the roof.
Very Strong Winds	Buildings and trees are badly damaged.

Winds can move slowly or quickly. Winds that move slowly are light winds. Winds that move more quickly are strong winds. Storm winds can be very strong. Very strong winds blow during hurricanes or tornadoes. Look at the wind chart. What happens when winds are light? What can happen when winds are strong? What might happen during very strong winds?

Clouds and Weather

There is water in the air. Water in the air can be in the form of a gas. Some water as a gas changes to a liquid or a solid when air cools. This water makes clouds. **Clouds** are large groups of tiny water drops, or pieces of ice in the air, or both.

There are many kinds of clouds. People like to look at them. They can tell what the weather will be from the clouds.

These white clouds are fluffy. The tops of fluffy clouds look like popcorn. The bottoms of these clouds are flat.

You may see fluffy clouds in fair weather. The weather may be sunny and warm. Have you ever looked for shapes in fluffy clouds?

Sometimes fluffy clouds get very dark. Rain may fall from these clouds. This rain does not last very long. It may start and end quickly.

   You may also see another kind of
cloud in fair weather. These clouds
look like feathers. They are very high
in the sky where the air is very cold.
Feathery clouds are made of small
pieces of ice. Rain does not fall from
these clouds. Look at the picture.
How do feathery clouds look different
from fluffy clouds?

Another kind of cloud covers the
sky like a blanket. These clouds
form thin layers. The layers are flat
and hang low in the sky.

The weather is not very sunny
when these clouds appear. Rain or
snow may fall for a long time. How
will you get ready for this weather?

Rain and snow are part of weather. Some places on Earth have rainy weather much of the year. Other places have little rain. Some places have snow in the winter. Some places never have snow at all.

Rain and snow are different forms of water. Rain is drops of liquid water. Snowflakes are tiny solid forms of water. Both fall from clouds to the ground. How could you measure how much rain or snow falls?

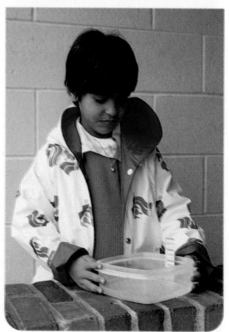

Science and Technology

Making Snow

Ski resorts need a lot of snow. People at ski resorts make the extra snow they need. They use snow-making machines. The temperature must be below 0°C to make snow. The machine mixes water with air. The cold air freezes the water into snow. Then the snow is shot out of the machine onto ski trails.

Air Temperature

The sun warms the air on Earth. Air is often warmer in the daytime than at night. Why do you think temperatures in summer are warmer than in winter?

The temperature of the air may change during the day. As air moves, air temperatures can change. The air can get warmer or cooler. Look at an outdoor thermometer. What is the temperature? How has it changed today?

Activity 7–2

How Do Temperatures Change?

Materials

outdoor thermometer   clock

pencil and paper

What to do

1. Measure the temperature of the air outdoors.
2. Record the temperature and the time you read it.
3. Measure the temperature of the air later the same day. Record it.
4. Measure the temperature 2 times every day for a week. Measure it at the same times each day.
5. Record each time and temperature.

What did you learn?

1. How did the temperatures change during the day?
2. How did the temperatures change during the week?

Studying temperatures and other changes in the air helps people know about weather. Weather is important to people. People choose the clothing they will wear each day when they know what the weather will be. What people choose to do can also depend on the weather. What would you wear on a warm, sunny day? What could you do on a cold, sunny day?

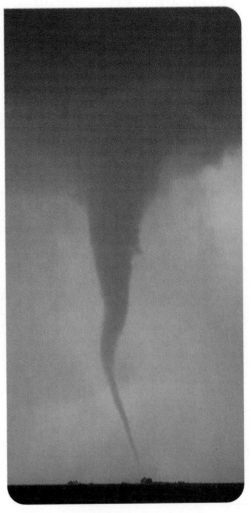

Scientists who observe weather learn about changes in the air. They observe changes in air temperature. They study how air moves. They study clouds and measure how much water is in the air. Scientists record what they learn about weather. How do you think scientists can tell us what kind of weather to expect?

Chapter 7 Review

Science I Know

- A thick layer of air covers Earth.
- Changes in the air cause weather.
- Rain and snow are forms of water in the air.

Science Words

Pick the best word for each sentence.

air   **weather**   **wind**   **wind vane**   **clouds**

1. Moving air outside is _____.

2. Large groups of tiny water drops or pieces of ice are called _____.

3. The layer of gases around Earth is called _____.

4. What is happening in the air outdoors is _____.

5. A _____ shows wind direction.

164

Questions to Answer

Use the pictures to help answer the questions.

1. What causes weather?

2. How can wind change?

3. How are clouds different?

4. How does air temperature change?

5. Why do people want to know about weather?

Something to Do

Set up a weather station. Observe wind direction and clouds. Measure rain or snow. Measure air temperatures. Tell about the weather.

Books to Read

Belinda's Hurricane by Elizabeth Winthrop
How the Weather Works by Peter Seymour
Winter Magic by Eveline Hasler

Chapter 8

Earth and the Sun

The sun is a star. Stars are very hot and give off light. The sun gives off light and heat. Why is the sun important to Earth?

Learning about planets

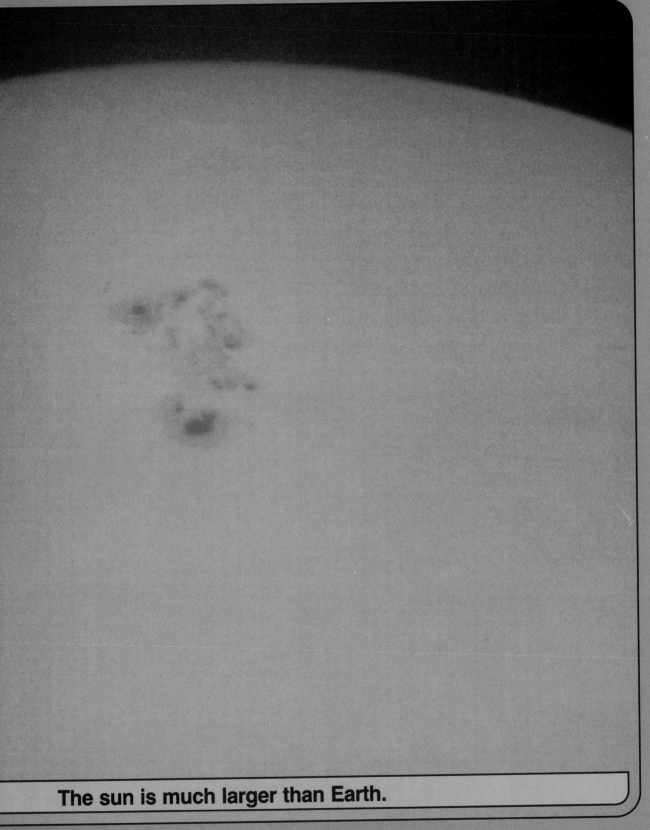

The sun is much larger than Earth.

The Sun and Its Planets

The sun is shaped like a ball.
Earth is like a ball, too. The
sun is a much bigger ball than
Earth. It seems smaller because it is
so far away.

Pretend you are going on a trip
that is as far away as the sun. If
you could ride on a jet plane, it
would take you about 18 years to
travel that far. If you left now, how
old would you be when you got there?

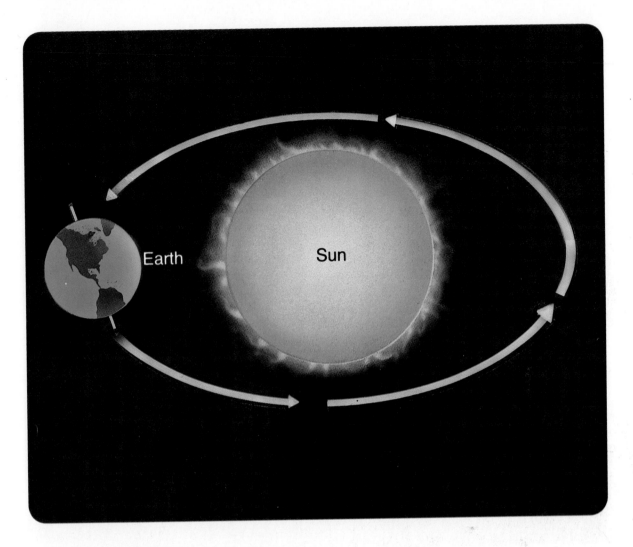

Both the sun and Earth move in space. Earth moves around the sun. Earth is a planet. A **planet** is an object in space that moves around the sun.

When Earth moves around the sun, it follows a path. The path Earth makes around the sun is called its **orbit**. Earth makes one orbit around the sun each year.

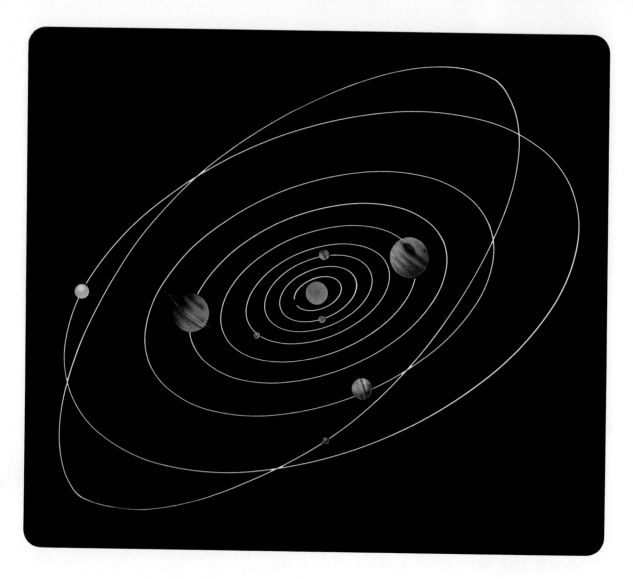

Earth is not the only planet in space. There are eight other large planets. They all make orbits around the sun.

Some of the planets are closer to the sun than Earth. Some are farther away. Which planet do you think takes the longest time to make an orbit around the sun?

People and Science

Studying the Planets

Julia Mair is the command operator for the Voyager Project. She is interested in learning about the landforms, gases, and measurements of different planets. The Voyager spacecraft uses cameras and instruments to gather this information and send it back to Earth. In August, 1989 Voyager II will be sending information back to Earth about the planet Neptune.

We can use a globe to learn more about Earth and the sun. A **globe** is a model of Earth. Look at the globe.

You can see that the globe is tilted. Earth is tilted in space, too. As Earth moves around the sun, parts of Earth are tilted toward the sun. These parts of Earth get more heat and light from the sun.

As Earth follows its path around the sun, different parts of Earth become tilted toward the sun. These parts of Earth then get more heat and light from the sun.

As Earth moves around the sun, the seasons change. A **season** is a certain time of year. Seasons change when the amount of light and heat from the sun changes.

During a summer season, part of Earth is warmer and has more daylight hours. During a winter season, part of Earth is cooler and has fewer daylight hours. When one part of Earth has summer, another part of Earth has winter. Name some other seasons of the year. Tell about these seasons. How many seasons are there where you live?

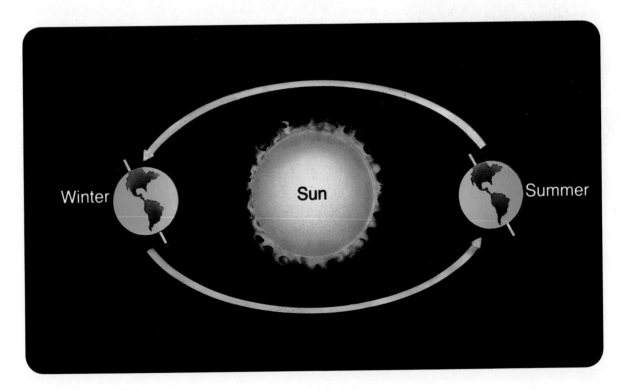

Activity 8–1

How Can You Use a Globe?

Materials

library books   globe   clay
three flag cutouts   tape
pencil and paper   toothpicks

What to do

1. Write North Pole, South Pole, and Home on the flag cutouts.
2. Tape the cutouts to toothpicks and stand them in small balls of clay.
3. Place the flags on the globe where they belong.
4. Find the line that goes around the middle of Earth. Look for countries near this line.
5. Find some warm and cool places on Earth.

What did you learn?

1. How is the temperature different in different places on Earth?
2. How does the temperature change during the year where you live?

All places on Earth do not get
the same amount of heat and light
from the sun. Places around the
middle of Earth get more sunlight and
heat. They are warm all year long.

Near the North and South Poles
it is cold much of the year. The
poles get less light and heat from
the sun. What is the land like near
the North and South Poles?

Day and Night

The sun seems to rise in the east each morning. During the day, the sun seems to move across the sky. It looks like it is high in the sky at about noon. The sun seems to set in the west each evening. The sun appears to move from east to west each day. But, the sun does not move, Earth turns.

Pretend you are on a merry-go-round. Look for a nearby object, like a tree. Pretend the tree is the sun and the merry-go-round is Earth. As you turn around, you see the tree from a different spot. For a while you cannot even see the tree at all. Earth is like a merry-go-round. We see the sun from a different spot as Earth turns.

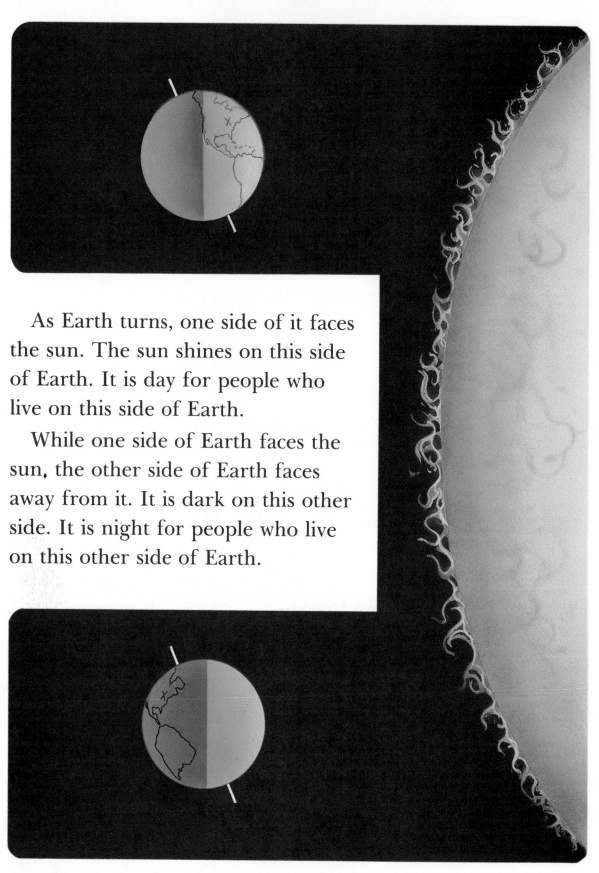

As Earth turns, one side of it faces the sun. The sun shines on this side of Earth. It is day for people who live on this side of Earth.

While one side of Earth faces the sun, the other side of Earth faces away from it. It is dark on this other side. It is night for people who live on this other side of Earth.

Earth keeps turning. Earth turns all the way around every 24 hours. A part of Earth is always having day while another part has night. When some people on Earth are waking up in the morning, other people are going to bed. Where on Earth is it night when you are having day?

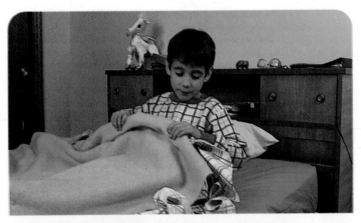

Light and Heat

Light from the sun travels. Some of this sunlight reaches Earth. When light from the sun reaches Earth, it changes to heat. Light and heat from the sun are important to all living things. Without heat and light, there would be no life on Earth.

Plants need heat and light to grow. Without heat and light, plants would stop growing. Animals that eat plants would have no food. They would die. Animals that eat plant-eating animals would not be able to find food. What would happen to these animals?

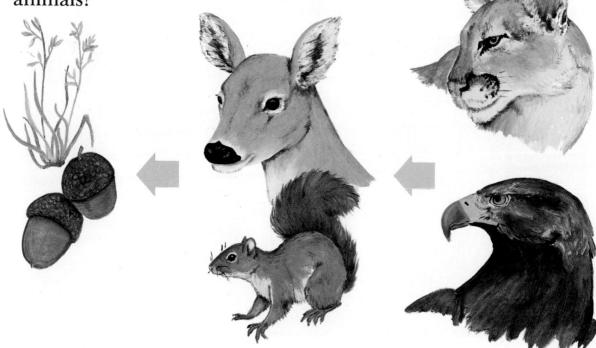

We must have sunlight to live. But, it can be harmful, too. You must never look right at the sun. It will hurt your eyes.

You should not stay out in the sun too long. You can get a sunburn. Sunburn is harmful to your skin. How can you protect yourself from sunburn?

Light and Shadows

Most objects do not give off light like the sun. Light bounces off these objects. The light bounces to our eyes. We see objects because of light. How do we see objects without light from the sun?

Light can pass through clear objects like windows. It can pass through water. Light can also pass through some objects that are not clear. What are some other objects that light can pass through?

Light cannot pass through all objects. Light cannot pass through books. Name other objects light cannot pass through.

A **shadow** is a dark place formed by an object that blocks light. Where have you seen shadows? How can you make a shadow?

Look at these shadows. Think about what objects blocked light to form these shadows. What do these shadows look like?

Activity 8–2

Materials

thread spool   rocks   scissors
pencil and paper   yarn   dowel rod

What to do

1. Stand the dowel rod in the spool of thread. Push it into a spot on the playground early in the morning.
2. Observe the shadow of the rod.
3. Tie a piece of yarn around the spool. Measure how long the shadow of the rod is. Cut the yarn.
4. Hold the yarn in place with a rock.
5. Measure the shadow of the rod 4 more times during the day.

What did you learn?

1. At what time of the day was the shadow longest?
2. At what time of the day was the shadow shortest?
3. Why did the shadows change?

186

Shadows change. Shadows in the
morning are longer. Shadows are
also longer in the afternoon.
Shadows change as Earth turns.
Suppose the sun were directly over
your head. What time of day would it be?
What would your shadow look like?

Voyage To The Moon

(Set is a curtain to which a cutout rocket has been attached. Light behind the curtain will make shadows of the action.)

NARRATOR: Astronauts, please board your ship. *(3 children as astronauts walk single file and place several objects including an umbrella and a toy animal behind the cutout. Then they stand behind the cutout.)* 10-9-8-7-6-5-4-3-2-1 Blast Off! *(Children shake rocket shake as during takeoff, they stop, and all is still.)*

ASTRONAUTS: Houston, Houston, help us soon, we're too heavy to reach the moon!

NARRATOR: Astronauts, lighten your load. Throw out something you won't need. *(A child picks up umbrella, opens it, and tosses it so that its shadow is seen on the curtain.)* 10-9-8-7-6-5-4-3-2-1 Blast Off! *(Children shake curtain, they stop, and all is still.)*

ASTRONAUTS: Houston, Houston, help us soon, we're too heavy to reach the moon!

NARRATOR: Astronauts, throw out something you won't need. *(A child picks up toy animal and tosses it to one side.)* 10-9-8-7-6-5-4-3-2-1 Blast Off! *(Children shake curtain, they stop, and all is still.)*

ASTRONAUTS: Houston, Houston, help us soon, we're too heavy to reach the moon! *(Continue "lightening the load" until last object has been tossed to one side. Then children shake curtain and raise it to make the rocket take off.)* Houston, Houston, the clock has struck noon, and now we're on our way to the moon!

189

Chapter 8 Review

- Earth and other planets move around the sun.
- Not all parts of Earth get the same amount of heat and light from the sun.
- Earth turns around once each day.
- Light cannot pass through some objects.

Science Words

Pick the best word for each sentence.

planet   orbit   globe   season   shadow

1. A certain time of year is a _____.
2. The path Earth makes around the sun is its _____.
3. An object that moves around the sun is a _____.
4. A model of Earth is a _____.
5. A dark place formed when objects block light is a _____.

Questions to Answer

Use the pictures to help answer the questions.

1. How does heat and light change during seasons?

2. What causes day and night?

3. Why is light and heat from the sun important?

4. Why do we have to be careful in the sun?

5. What objects can light pass through?

6. Why do shadows change?

Something to Do

Cut animal shapes out of construction paper. Tape them to pencils. Put them in front of light. Make the animals shadow dance.

Books to Read

Bear Shadow by Frank Asch
Comets by Franklyn M. Branley
The Seasons by David Lambert

Chapter 9

Plants Change

There are many kinds of plants. Plants grow to many sizes, shapes, and colors. What do you know about plants? How are these plants different from each other?

Plants need water.

Plants grow in many different places.

Plants Grow

Plants are living things. They need food, water, and air. They change as they grow.

Most plants need light to grow. They grow when the air and soil are the right temperatures. Why do you think many plants begin to grow in the spring?

Many plants grow in soil. They take in water from soil. How do plants take in water? How else is soil useful to plants?

Scientists have been studying plants for a long time. They have learned how plants get food. Scientists found out that many plants make their own food. Plants do not get food from the soil.

Green plants make their own food. They make food in their leaves when there is light. Green plants also use water and air to make food.

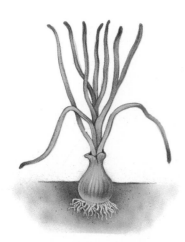

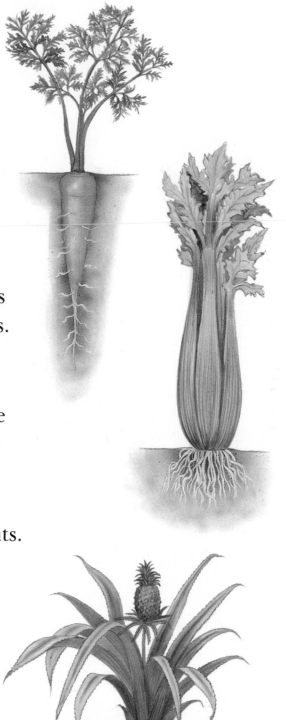

Most green plants make extra food. This food is stored for the plant to use later. Different plants store food in different plant parts.

Some plants store food in their roots. Some store food in their stems or leaves. Other plants have food stored in their fruit. Many plants store food in their seeds.

Look at these pictures. They show where food is stored in plants. What parts of plants do you see?

Activity 9–1

Where Do Plants Store Food?

Materials

2 potatoes (1 cut in half)
2 onions (1 cut in half)
paper towels
pencil and paper

What to do

1. Observe the cut onion and potato.
2. Draw a picture of what you observe.
3. Place a whole onion and a whole potato on paper towels and put them in a sunny spot.
4. Observe the potato and the onion for 3 weeks. Draw what you observe.

What did you learn?

1. How did the potato change?
2. How did the onion change?
3. Why do you think they began to change?

Many plants grow from seeds. Seeds have stored food. Young plants use this food when they begin to grow. What are some plants that grow from seeds?

Some plants can grow from bulbs. A **bulb** is a short stem covered with thick leaves. It grows underground. Bulbs have stored food in their leaves. Onions are bulbs. Tulips grow from bulbs. Tell about other plants that have bulbs.

Some plants live for a very long time. Many trees grow to be very old. A few live to be hundreds of years old. How old do you think the oldest tree is?

Some plants live for a short time. They begin to grow when the air and ground around them get warm. They make flowers and seeds. These plants live only until the weather turns cold. Why do new plants grow when the air and ground get warm again?

Where Plants Live

Plants live and grow in many different places. They grow where their needs are met. Some plants need lots of sunlight to grow. Others grow best in the shade. Some plants need a lot of water. Some do not.

Plants grow in different temperatures. Some grow where the air and soil are very warm. Others grow where it is cooler. What kinds of plants grow where you live? What are their needs?

The place where a plant lives and grows is called its **habitat.** A habitat can be an ocean or a desert. It can be the top of a mountain. Think of where plants live. What are some other habitats?

Many plants can live in only one kind of habitat. Plants that live in the ocean use salt water. Saltwater plants could not live in a forest.

Some plants are able to live in a desert. A desert is very dry and hot. Many desert plants can store water to use when it does not rain. What desert plant can you name? How can you find out if it stores water?

Some plants grow near the tops of mountains. It can be very cold at the top of a mountain. Many mountain plants are very small. They grow close to the ground where it is warmer.

Packaging Seeds

Joan Brown works for a seed company. She packages seeds that will be sold in stores. The machine counts the number of seeds in each package.

A picture of the grown plant is shown on the front of the package. Directions for planting are given on the back. The directions tell how to plant the seeds and when the seeds can be grown.

Plants can be put into groups. Plants that grow and change in the same way are put in the same group. One plant group is called mosses. A **moss** is a small green plant with no flowers that grows close to the ground. Mosses grow in damp shady places.

Another group of plants is called ferns. A **fern** has no flowers and has leaves like feathers. Most ferns grow where it is very moist and shady.

Have you ever observed trees? How are trees different from each other? Some trees have leaves shaped like needles. These trees grow cones. The cones have seeds.

Plants that grow cones belong to a group called conifers. A **conifer** has no flowers and grows seeds in cones. A pine tree is a conifer. The leaves of most conifers stay green all year long. Tell about the leaves on different kinds of conifers.

Most trees that have wide flat leaves make seeds from flowers. These trees are part of a group of plants called flowering plants. There are many kinds of flowering plants.

Flowering plants make fruits. The fruits have seeds. All flowering plants can make new plants from seeds. How many plants can you name that make flowers? Tell about their flowers and seeds.

Activity 9–2

How Are Tree Leaves Different?

Materials

hand lens   manila paper
yarn   tree leaves
crayons   books about trees
pencil and paper

What to do

1. Observe each leaf with a hand lens.
2. Trace around each leaf on manila paper.
3. Use the tree books and find out which tree each leaf comes from.
4. Write each tree name under the leaf that belongs to each kind of tree. Draw its seed.
5. Use yarn and make a book with your leaf pages.

What did you learn?

1. How are tree leaves different from each other?
2. What are other ways trees are different from each other?
3. How are trees different from other plants?

Changes in the Seasons

Most plants change when the seasons change. Plants change because temperatures and the amount of sunlight change during each season.

In spring, the air and ground get warm. Buds begin to open. Buds open into leaves or flowers. Seeds and bulbs sprout. New leaves push up through the ground. What kind of weather do you expect in the spring? How does this weather help plants grow?

Summer is the season that follows spring. There are many more hours of sunlight in the summer. Temperatures get warmer. Plants grow bigger. They grow more leaves and flowers. Many plants grow fruit.

Some people grow flowers or vegetables during the summer. Farmers stay busy growing plants for food. People work to help plants grow better. How can people help plants grow better? What plants do you like to grow or eat?

Autumn follows summer. Autumn is another name for fall. Plants form seeds in autumn. Many leaves on trees change color and fall to the ground.

People are busy in autumn. People rake leaves. They pick fruit and pull vegetables. Farmers harvest food crops. What kinds of plants do farmers harvest in autumn? How does the temperature change?

Winter is the coldest season of the year. It follows autumn. There are not as many hours of sunlight. Some plants stop growing and die.

In winter, some trees that lose their leaves look dead. They are resting. They are growing very slowly. When spring returns, they will begin to grow quickly again.

Some people live where it is warm all year. Instead of having four seasons, they have two. One season is very dry. The other season is wet. During the wet season, a lot of rain falls and plants grow very fast.

Some people live where it is cold all year. Only a few plants grow where it is very cold. Cold places have some days when the sun warms the air and soil. Plants can then grow. Most days during the year there is not much light or heat. Where on Earth could you find some very cold places?

Science and Technology

Picking Cotton

Cotton is an important crop. It can be used for making cotton cloth, stuffing mattresses, and for medical supplies. Cotton seeds are important in the making of salad and cooking oils.

At one time cotton was harvested by hand. Now, machines save people many hours of work by picking the cotton. After the cotton is picked, a machine called a cotton gin pulls the cotton fibers from the seeds.

Chapter 9 Review

Science I Know

- Green plants use light to make their own food.
- Plants live in different habitats.
- Most plants change when the seasons change.

Science Words

Pick the best word for each sentence.

bulb   habitat   moss   fern   conifer

1. A short stem covered with leaves is a _____.

2. A plant that grows its seeds in cones is a _____.

3. The place a plant lives is its _____.

4. A _____ has no flowers and lives close to the ground.

5. A plant that has leaves like feathers and grows no flowers is a _____.

Questions to Answer

Use the picture to help answer the questions.

1. What do plants need to grow?
2. Where do green plants store food?
3. What kinds of plants do you see?
4. How will these plants change?
5. What plant parts could living things eat?

Something to Do

Draw some faces on eggshell halves. Fill the shells with soil. Plant some rye grass seeds. Water the seeds. Trim your eggheads when needed.

Books to Read

Look at Trees by Rena K. Kirkpatrick
The One Hundred Year Old Cactus by Anita Holmes
Sophie and Jack Help Out by Judy Taylor

Chapter 10

Our Environment Changes

People need water and air. They need other living things. They need things that are not living. What do you need to live?

Living in the country

Large cities have air and water, too.

What Is Around You

You live in an environment. Your **environment** is everything around you. Land, water, and air are around you. Plants and animals are around you, too. Everything that is around you, indoors and outdoors, is part of your environment.

Anything that people need can be found in the environment. People need food, water, and air. People need clothing and a place to live. Where do people find the things they need in their environment?

Anything in the environment that people use is a **resource.** What do you use at school? Any object that you use at school is a resource. Your books, pencils, paper, and crayons are all resources. What resources do you use for art?

There are many resources in the environment. Light and heat from the sun are resources. Land, water, and air are resources. Plants and animals are resources, too. We need the resources we find around us.

Some resources are found under the ground. Coal, oil, and natural gas are formed under the ground. It took millions of years for these resources to form. How do people use coal, oil, and natural gas?

220

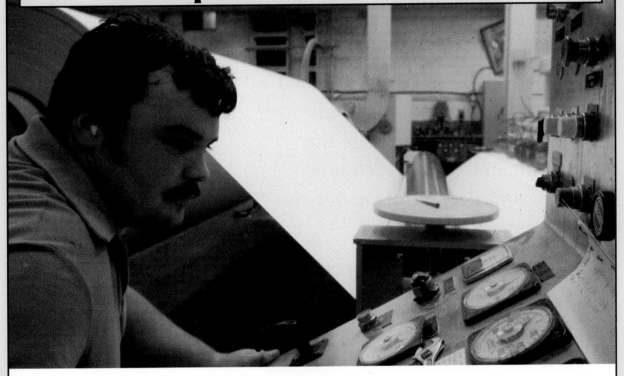

Papermaker

George Welch works for a paper company. Paper is made from trees. Trees that are 20 to 30 years old are ground up into little chips. After the chips are made into pulp, the pulp is made into paper.

Tree bark is not used in making paper, but it is not wasted. After the bark is stripped from each tree, the paper company burns it to make heat. The heat runs the machines in the paper factory.

Changes in the Environment

Our environment does not stay the same. It changes. We can observe some of these changes.

We can observe changes caused by weather. Very strong winds and heavy rain can change the environment quickly. Tell how storms and floods can change the environment.

We can observe some changes in the environment that happen slowly. Some changes in the environment take many years to happen. Look at the pictures.

Some plants take many years to grow. As they grow, they get bigger and taller. Trees that get very tall block sunlight from smaller plants. Plants that need shade begin to grow. The environment changes as plants grow.

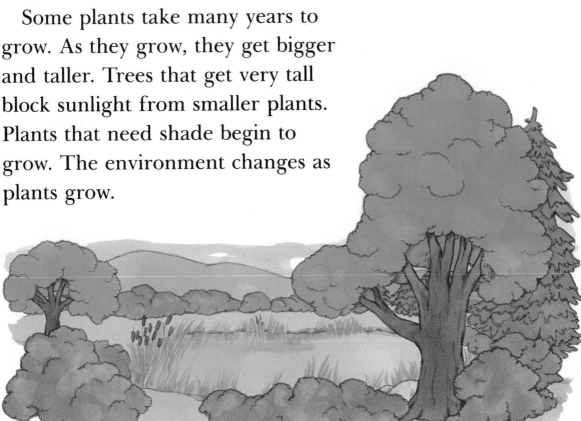

People change the environment
in many ways. Some changes
people make in the environment
are helpful.

The land in the picture was
changed. People needed to keep
the river from flooding. They built
a dam. A lake formed behind the
dam. How does the dam keep the
river from flooding? How do you
think people use the lake?

People change the environment when they use resources. People use resources that are under the ground. They dig mines to get coal out of the ground. They drill wells to get oil and natural gas.

Sometimes people make many changes in the environment to get the resources they need. Look at the pictures. These people are mining coal. When they were done, how did they change the environment back again? What would the environment look like if these people had not cared about it?

Some changes people make to the environment are harmful. Air, water, and land can become polluted. **Pollution** makes our environment dirty.

Smoke and gases from cars and chimneys cause air pollution. Air pollution can be harmful to both plants and animals. Why do plants and animals need clean air?

Animals and plants need clean water. How did the water in the pictures become polluted? What might happen to the plants and animals that live in the water?

Look at how land can become polluted. People who do not care about our land throw litter. **Litter** is trash that people scatter about our environment. Why do you think people throw litter?

Activity 10–1

How Can You Change Your Environment?

Materials

2 sheets manila paper
crayons   pencil and paper

What to do

1. Choose a part of your school that needs to be cleaned up.
2. Plan how the environment can be changed.
3. Work together with your class to clean up the part of your school you chose.
4. Draw a picture of the environment before and after you clean it up.

What did you learn?

1. What part of your school did you clean up?
2. Why did you choose this part to clean?
3. What can be done to keep this environment clean?

Science and Technology

Plants at Work

Water hyacinths are flowers that have important uses. The water hyacinths are grown in large tanks of water. The water contains sewage. Sometimes the water can contain garbage. As the water hyacinths grow, they clean the water in the tanks. The plants grow quickly and need to be harvested weekly. The cut plants can be used to make cattle feed.

Saving Our Environment

Changes in the environment can cause problems for living things. Think what happens to plants and animals after a forest fire. Fire kills many animals. It destroys trees and other plants. Animals that do not die need plants for food and homes. It takes time for new plants to grow. The animals must find ways to live in the new environment or die.

Pollution causes many problems
for living things. Pollution can poison
plants and animals. It can poison the
habitats of plants and animals.

Because of pollution, some plants
and animals are in danger of
becoming extinct. Find out which
animals and plants are in danger
because of pollution. How can
people stop pollution?

Activity 10-2

What Do You Throw Away?

Materials

3 large plastic food bags
masking tape   pencil and paper

What to do

1. Use tape and label each bag paper, plastic, and metal.
2. Tape the bags to your desk.
3. Each day, throw away your used paper in the bag marked paper. Throw plastic and metal away in the other two bags.
4. At the end of the day, see what you have thrown away into each bag.
5. Record what you throw away each day.

What did you learn?

1. What did you throw away?
2. Could you have used any of these objects more wisely? Which ones?
3. Which objects could you use again?

There are some laws that protect our environment. These laws were made to keep our environment clean and safe. Some laws protect our resources. What law would you make to protect our environment?

We can save our environment by using resources wisely. Using resources wisely is called **conservation.** We must learn to practice conservation. How do you practice conservation?

Chapter 10 Review

Science I Know

- Everything around us is part of the environment.
- Living things need the resources in the environment.
- Changes in the environment can be helpful or harmful.
- People must take care of their environment.

Science Words

Pick the best word for each sentence.

environment   resource   pollution   litter   conservation

1. Trash scattered about the environment is called _____.

2. Anything we use in the environment is a _____.

3. Everything around us is the _____.

4. Using resources wisely is _____.

5. Resources are made dirty by _____.

Use the picture to answer the questions.

1. What is in your environment?
2. How can the environment change?
3. How does the environment become polluted?
4. How can people practice conservation?

Something to Do

Find out if there are places in your town that are polluted. Find out who is taking care of the problem. Choose a way to help take care of the problem.

Books to Read

Anno's Flea Market by Mitsumasa Anno
Endangered Animals by Lynn M. Stone
Fly Away Free by Joan Hewett

GLOSSARY

The glossary is a list of your science words in ABC order. The phrase after the word tells you what the word means. In *italics* you will read a sentence using the word.

Look for the word **"bulb."** Read the phrase that tells what your science word means. Read the sentence using the word **"bulb."**

A

air a layer of gases around Earth that we can feel but cannot smell or taste: *The air feels cold today.*

amphibian an animal that can live both on land and in water: *A frog is an amphibian.*

B

baby teeth the first set of teeth: *The little boy has all of his baby teeth.*

bird an animal with feathers and a beak: *The bird was able to fly.*

bulb a short underground stem with thick leaves: *We will plant our tulip bulb next autumn.*

C

centimeter unit used to measure how long or how wide something is: *I will use my centimeter ruler.*

clouds objects formed by tiny water drops or ice pieces floating in the air: *The storm clouds moved quickly across the sky.*

conifer a plant with no flowers that grows seeds in cones: *A pine tree is a conifer.*

conservation using resources wisely: *Conservation will help us have a better world.*

D

degree a unit on a thermometer: *It is only one degree cooler today than it was yesterday.*

E

energy being able to work or play: *Food gives us energy to grow.*

environment everything around you: *We should take care of our environment.*

exercise moving your body to keep it healthy: *Riding a bicycle is good exercise.*

extinct plants and animals that can no longer be found alive: *Dinosaurs are extinct animals.*

F

fern a plant with no flowers and leaves like feathers: *A fern sometimes grows in the woods.*

fish animals that live in water and take in air through gills: *Fish use their fins and tails to move in the water.*

fossil a print or part of plants or animals that lived long ago: *We found a fossil in the rocks.*

fuel something that is burned to make heat: *The fireplace uses wood for fuel.*

G

glacier a large body of ice that moves: *A glacier can carry rocks and soil with it as it moves.*

globe a model of Earth: *A globe is shaped like a ball.*

H

habitat the place where a plant lives and grows: *A field is the habitat of many wildflowers.*

heat what makes objects feel warm: *You can feel the heat from the sun on a sunny day.*

I

insect an animal with six legs and three main body parts: *A fly is a kind of insect.*

L

landforms different land shapes on the face of Earth: *Mountains and plains are landforms.*

liter a unit used to measure volume: *The four children shared a liter of juice.*

litter trash scattered about the environment: *We should clean up litter whenever we see it.*

Keep Our Land Beautiful

M

mammal an animal with a bony skeleton and skin covered with hair: *A tiger is a mammal.*

meter a unit used to measure how long or how wide an object is: *A meter is 100 centimeters long.*

moss a very small, green plant with no flowers: *Moss sometimes grows on trees.*

N

noise sound that is not pleasant to hear: *There was very little noise in the classroom.*

O

orbit the path a planet follows around the sun: *Earth makes one orbit around the sun each year.*

P

permanent teeth the second set of teeth: *You will get a set of permanent teeth after you lose your baby teeth.*

pitch the highness or lowness of a sound: *The tuba has a low pitch.*

planet an object in space that moves around the sun: *Earth is a planet.*

pollution   dirty or harmful material in the environment: *Smoke is one kind of air pollution.*

R

reptile   an animal with dry, scaly skin and a bony skeleton: *We saw reptile eggs in the sand.*

resource   what is used in the environment: *We should use any resource wisely.*

S

scale   an instrument used to measure weight: *The girl weighed the oranges on a scale.*

season   one of the four time units of a year: *Summer is a warm season.*

shadow   a dark place formed by an object that blocks light: *The teacher made a shadow on the wall.*

skill   something you can learn to do: *Cooking is a fun skill to learn.*

T

temperature   a measure of how warm something is: *The temperature of food gets higher when it is in a hot oven.*

thermometer   an instrument used to measure how hot or cold something is: *We use a thermometer to find the temperature.*

V

vibrate to move back and forth: *The drum will vibrate when you hit it.*

volume a measure of how much an object can hold: *A bucket has a larger volume than a cup.*

W

weather what happens to the air outdoors: *Weather changes with the seasons.*

weight a measure of how heavy an object is: *The nurse will check the child's weight.*

wind moving air: *The wind was blowing hard today.*

wind vane instrument that shows wind direction: *There is a wind vane on the roof.*

Index

W

PHOTO CREDITS